AF374391

The Entrepreneur Success Formula

How the Top 10% Escape the

ACHIEVEMENT TRAP

and Build a Life They Actually Want

GREG SLAUGHTER

The Entrepreneur Success Formula

© Copyright 2026 Greg Slaughter All rights reserved.

No part of this publication may be reproduced, distributed, or transmitted in any form or by any means—including photocopying, recording, or other electronic or mechanical methods—without the prior written permission of the publisher, except in the case of brief quotations embodied in critical reviews and certain other noncommercial uses permitted by copyright law.

Although the author and publisher have made every effort to ensure that the information in this book was correct at press time, they do not assume and hereby disclaim any liability to any party for any loss, damage, or disruption caused by errors or omissions, whether such errors or omissions result from negligence, accident, or any other cause.

Adherence to all applicable laws and regulations—including international, federal, state, and local laws governing professional licensing, business practices, advertising, and all other aspects of doing business in the U.S., Canada, or any other jurisdiction—is the sole responsibility of the reader and consumer.

Neither the author nor the publisher assumes any responsibility or liability whatsoever on behalf of the consumer or reader of this material. Any perceived slight of any individual or organization is purely unintentional.

The resources in this book are provided for informational purposes only and should not be used to replace the specialized training and professional judgment of a health care or mental health care professional.

Please always consult a trained professional before making any decision regarding treatment of yourself or others. Neither the author nor the publisher can be held responsible for the use of the information provided within this book.

For more information, email: Support@theNLSinstitute.com

ISBN: 979-8-9945586-0-7 - Paperback

ISBN: 979-8-9945586-1-4 - Hardback

ISBN: 979-8-9945586-2-1 - Audiobook

ISBN: 979-8-9945586-3-8 - eBook

Published by Next Level Success Institute, Inc.

A Gift for Readers

Take the Free Success Diagnostic (4–7 minutes)

Pinpoint your fastest path to momentum—before you start the book.

In a few minutes you'll get a personalized snapshot across five essentials:

- **Ownership & Control**—are you leading your calendar or reacting to it?

- **Congruence**—are your goals and daily actions pointed at the life you actually want?

- **Capacity**—the skills & self-mastery to execute under pressure

- **Consistency**—systems & routines that make progress automatic

- **Collaboration**—people & support that multiply results

You'll receive:

- **Instant scorecard + your #1 leverage move** for this week

- **Clear focus areas** to accelerate results without burnout

- **Optional email copy** of your results so you can track progress over time

You'll meet this full framework in the chapters ahead—this just gives you a head start.

Start the diagnostic free:

https://www.MySuccessDiagnostic.com

Or scan this QR code to access instantly:

Foreword

Most success narratives are built on sacrifice—work harder, give more, and postpone life until some future milestone. After years of working closely with entrepreneurs across a wide range of industries, I've seen this mindset repeated again and again—and I've also seen where it leads. Achievement may increase, but fulfillment often doesn't.

Greg Slaughter challenges that belief.

What makes Greg's work different is its focus on alignment. This book shows how to create the life you want by bringing who you are, how you live, and what you're building into sync. When values, decisions, and daily actions are aligned, growth becomes more natural and far less exhausting.

I've had the opportunity to see Greg's approach up close, and what stands out is that it isn't theoretical. He doesn't promote success that comes at the expense of health, relationships, or peace of mind. Instead, he demonstrates how clarity and alignment can support meaningful success across all areas of life—without regret.

This is not a book about sacrificing more. It's about choosing better. It's about building success in a way that actually supports the life you want to live, rather than competing with it.

For anyone who has achieved progress yet feels something is missing—or who wants to pursue success without losing themselves along the way—this book offers a clear and grounded path forward.

— Eddie Wilson
CEO, Collective Influence

Dedication

I dedicate this book in honor of **Ashley and Narissa**, my two daughters whom I never had the opportunity to meet or share a life with.

I miss you both more with each passing year, and I want you to know—you will never be forgotten.

You have inspired me to write this book for the busy entrepreneurs of the world—so they can build not just a successful business, but a life they truly love at the same time. My deepest hope is that your loss will help millions never take their families—or their lives—for granted.

Acknowledgments

To **my wife, Kim**—

You inspired me to change my life, which ultimately led to the discovery of the Entrepreneur Success Formula shared in these pages. None of this would have been possible without you and your unwavering support. Thank you for believing in me.

To **Duncan Wierman**—

You gave me hope when I needed it most. When I was at my worst, your kindness and willingness to help restored my belief that trustworthy people still existed. Your support gave me the confidence and motivation to keep going. I will never forget that.

To **my dad, Jerry**—

As I prepared to write this book, you passed away. But the values, discipline, and foundation you gave me as a child helped shape the man I am today. Thank you for being part of my journey.

Contents

Read This First

You've Had Some Success. You've already accomplished what most only talk about. You started a business. You've seen some wins. You've built momentum. You're not lost and you're definitely not a beginner.

But now you want more.

More isn't selfish—it's a signal. It means you're ready for what's next.

More growth in your business.

More revenue.

More control over your time.

More clarity on what actually moves the needle.

More freedom—without having to hustle harder to get it.

More energy for the rest of your life.

More fulfillment.

More fun.

More passion in your relationships.

More peace of mind, knowing nothing important is being neglected.

You're not chasing more for the sake of it—you're pursuing a life that *feels* like success, one you love living.

You didn't build a business to be trapped by it. This book is your path to freedom—and to having more. It is written for entrepreneurs who've already achieved some success and are ready to go further and faster, without burnout, stalls, or sacrifice. It offers a proven roadmap to maximize your results, your time, and your life.

You don't need to work harder—you need to work *aligned*. This isn't about doing more; it's about doing what works— the way the top 10% of entrepreneurs operate. They aren't grinding harder; they're operating differently. Once you apply what you're about to learn, they're no longer ahead of you— you're in the same game, playing to win.

You've already proven you can work hard. Now it's time to win smartly.

Don't just scale your business—scale your life. You don't need a hundred new strategies; you need the *right system*.

Keep what's working. But if you're ready to upgrade how you operate, unlock faster business growth, and build a life that feels as good as it looks—**this book is your roadmap.**

If you've ever felt like you're spinning your wheels—working hard but not getting as far as you thought you would—this is where that changes. What you're about to read isn't theory; it's a blueprint for real-world results you can actually live.

To ensure this isn't just another book you read—but one you *implement*—I've built in practical tools designed to get you results.

First, by the end of Chapter 2, you'll take a quick 4–7 minute clarity check: the *Entrepreneur Success Diagnostic*. It's a powerful tool that gives you an instant snapshot of your strengths and the areas that may be holding you back. You'll get your results online (and a printable version in the appendix), and I'll guide you step-by-step on how to use it.

Second, if you ever get stuck along the way, don't worry. I've created a 24/7 *AI Success Strategist*—trained on the full *4C² Success Formula*, the *SUCCESS Operating System*, and this book—to answer your questions, help you apply what you're learning, and keep you moving forward anytime you need it.

Access it anytime at https://www.NextLevelSuccessInstitute.com/ai

Or scan the QR code below:

Let's get started—more growth, more freedom, more of you begins now.

Introduction

What If You've Been Chasing the Wrong Kind of Success?

Just after 6 a.m. on a September morning in 2010, my wife, Kim, shook me awake. Her hands were trembling. Her voice cracked as she whispered, *"I'm sorry… I'm so sorry… I need to tell you something…"*

At first, I thought I was dreaming. Then I saw her face—pale, soaked in tears—and I knew this was real. And bad.

I'd been with my wife for sixteen years, but I had never seen her like this. She was crying so hard she could barely breathe. I sat up quickly, my heart racing, my mind jumping straight to the darkest corners.

At the time, we were barely surviving. The Great Recession had crushed our finances. Our real estate business was bleeding thousands of dollars every month. Our home was in foreclosure. Someone had stolen $20,000 from us just a few months earlier. Our savings were gone. We had no income, no backup plan, and no way out. For the first time in my life, my health was slipping. I didn't know how much more I could take—and now this.

She looked away. After several attempts, through broken breaths, she finally said, *"I opened a couple credit cards behind your back… and maxed them out. We owe $85,000 on them."*

Inside, I shattered. I felt betrayed, crushed, and lost. It wasn't just about the money—I knew bankruptcy was coming. It was the trust. The last thread I thought I had. Suddenly, I felt completely alone, with no idea how to move forward.

What I didn't know then was that this moment would become the greatest gift of my life. That morning was my wake-up call—the one that would lead me to the formula you're about to learn. The very formula that rebuilt my business, my marriage, and my life.

Up until that moment, I had done everything I thought I was supposed to do. I worked hard. I climbed the ladder. I sacrificed. I followed every "success" blueprint from books, seminars, and coaching programs. But not one of them prepared me for this.

No one tells you that chasing success the wrong way can cost you everything that matters most. I was forced to re-evaluate everything I had built—and realize just how fragile it all was.

The truth was hard to admit: I had spent my entire adult life chasing success. I started managing a McDonald's at 19. I climbed the corporate ladder and eventually oversaw training for hundreds of restaurants and thousands of managers across seven states. In 2002, I left to build a real estate business that, by 2006, had made us millionaires—at least on paper.

I won awards. I got applause. From the outside, I looked successful. But inside, I was sacrificing everything that truly mattered.

I worked 12-16 hours a day, six or seven days a week, for more than 25 years. I skipped birthdays, holidays, and game nights—all in the name of *"someday."* I convinced myself that once I *"made it,"* my wife would understand the sacrifices and my future kids would appreciate them. I kept putting off life—joy, health, presence, connection—all for the illusion of future freedom.

Even when we lost our full-term daughter, Narissa, in 2000, I didn't stop to grieve; I worked harder. I called it strength— what successful people do. But the truth, I was avoiding pain by chasing achievement.

And yet, after all that, there I was—forty-four years old, broke, exhausted, emotionally bankrupt, filing for actual bankruptcy. No house. Borrowing money from our parents for the security deposit on a tiny home. No joy. No peace. No kids. A marriage in ruins.

All those years of work and sacrifice… for what? I had built a life full of achievements—but I didn't feel successful. Not even close.

That's when the question hit me—the one that changed everything:

Do I want a life of achievements… or a life of success?

That question didn't just make me rethink my work; it forced me to confront the truth that I didn't have forever—and I had already spent decades chasing *"someday."* I realized I didn't just want to succeed. I wanted to live in a way that, if my time came tomorrow, I could look back without a single major regret.

No more putting off experiences. No more sacrificing relationships. No more trading my health, peace, or joy for the illusion of future freedom. I wanted to win in business *and* live fully now—so that when my last day comes, I'll know I didn't waste the days I had.

That moment changed everything.

From that point forward, I decided to live a life of true success— success in every area: my finances, my business, my marriage, my relationships, my health, my joy, all at once. I would no longer sacrifice one part of my life to succeed in another. I didn't want *"someday"* anymore. I wanted *"now."*

I didn't want to grind 80 hours a week ever again. I didn't want to be *"efficient"* only to end up more overwhelmed. I told myself, *"There's got to be a way to achieve massive success— without losing everything in the process."*

I wanted to live, love, thrive, and succeed—in business and in every area of life.

I had no idea how, but I was determined to figure it out.

What followed was a relentless search. I studied the habits of the most successful entrepreneurs—not just the rich ones, but the fulfilled ones. I wanted to know what they did differently.

Not just how they thought, but what they did—the consistent action that produced extraordinary results. I studied their skills, strategies, systems, and tools, looking for what I could apply to achieve the same kind of transformation.

Then I began to apply what I'd learned—letting go of the way I'd always operated and replacing them with the new principles and practices. It wasn't instant, and not everything worked right away. But with steady effort, the results came.

Over the next nine years, I rebuilt my life from zero. I achieved business success and financial freedom—starting from bankruptcy and rebuilding a thriving real estate business that gave us our life back. We went from no income and foreclosure notices to consistent cash flow, time freedom, and peace of mind. It wasn't just about money; it was about taking charge of our future.

I rebuilt my marriage and this time, I did it right. We'd originally married on a whim in Las Vegas, without family or a real ceremony. But on our anniversary, I got down on one knee among rose petals and re-proposed—the way I should have the first time. I told Kim to plan the wedding of her dreams, with her dad walking her down the aisle. And she did. Surrounded by family and friends, we renewed our vows in the most meaningful, emotional, and unforgettable way possible. It marked a brand-new chapter for both of us.

I improved my health—regaining energy, strength, and vitality for the first time in years. I restored my relationship with my parents, built deep new friendships, and traveled across all fifty states and all seven continents. I experienced more joy, peace, and fun than ever before, and I did it all in those nine years, simultaneously, without crazy hours, burnout, or sacrificing what mattered most.

I've now dedicated my life to helping others do the same. I'm a Success Strategist and the founder of the Next-Level Success Institute, where I empower entrepreneurs to live their 'life of success'—achieving and enjoying extraordinary results in business and every area of life, without sacrificing what truly matters. What you're reading is the culmination of that work.

So what changed?

What separates the most successful entrepreneurs—those who achieve extraordinary results and love the lives they've built—from the 90% who stay stuck in the Achievement Loop, constantly chasing more but never feeling like it's enough?

I discovered a consistent pattern: one non-negotiable foundation, plus four aligned elements. When these five components are in place, anyone can accelerate success far faster than they expect.

I call it the **Entrepreneur 4C² Success Formula**. It's a powerful, proven formula that works in any area you apply it—business, relationships, health, or life. The foundation is simple but transformative: **take ownership and control** and live a 'You First' Life—a process that changes everything.

Once that foundation is in place, you implement four aligned core elements:

- **Create Congruence**
- **Cultivate Your Capacity**
- **Commit to Consistency**
- **Champion Collaboration**

Each element is powerful on its own—but when aligned on that foundation, they unlock an entirely different level of success. Not just financial success, but *next-level success* in every part of your life.

And here's the part most people don't believe until they experience it themselves: when applied together, the *4C² Success Formula produces extraordinary results fast.* Most people assume real transformation takes years of grinding and sacrifice. It doesn't. You just need the right formula—and this is it.

I know how frustrating it feels to do all the right things—grow the business, check every box—but still feel like something's missing. That quiet sense that success should feel *different.* That it should feel better.

You're not crazy. And you're not alone. I've been there—and so have the most successful entrepreneurs I work with today.

Whether you're an entrepreneur growing your business, a leader carrying the weight of responsibility, or a high achiever chasing more—this book is for you. I wrote it for those who feel stuck despite doing all the "right" things—for the ones who secretly wonder if it's even possible to win in business and live a life they love.

It is.

This book isn't just my story—it's your roadmap to a new way of succeeding. If you've been pouring everything into your business but still aren't getting the results or the freedom you deserve, you're not alone. And it's not your fault. You've just been sold the wrong version of success.

You don't need to sacrifice more. You don't need to wait for *"someday."* You just need a better process—one that works for you, not against you.

The $4C^2$ Success Formula is that process—and when you apply it fully, it will take you to next-level success faster than you ever thought possible. You'll see part of yourself in my story, and by the end of this book, you'll have a practical system to create next-level success in your business and every other area of your life—without burnout or regret.

In the chapters ahead, I'll guide you through laying the foundation and mastering each of the four elements. You'll learn how to apply them and use the tools to finally create the level of success and life you were meant to live—not *someday*, but *now*.

This is your invitation to stop chasing a life of achievements—and finally start living a life of success.

Before we dive in, I want to challenge you. This process works. I've seen it transform the lives of entrepreneurs across every background, industry, and stage of business. It doesn't matter where you live, what you sell, or who you are—it's about implementing a proven formula. When you do, you'll achieve results faster than most people believe possible.

That said, some of what you'll read here will challenge what you've been taught. Much of it may feel counterintuitive—even uncomfortable. You may have spent years believing one way of doing things, only to discover the exact opposite was true all along.

So I ask you now: are you willing to question what you think you know? Can you stay open to a new way of working, living, and leading?

This book wasn't written to tell you what you *want* to hear. It was written to tell you what you *need* to hear—if you're truly ready to create next-level success.

And make no mistake—you won't just be reading. You'll be doing. This is a *workbook*. A *guide*. A process to follow. Each section includes reflections, actions, and tools to help you immediately implement and get results.

But I won't sugar-coat it—most people won't finish. One study found that fewer than 20% of people ever complete the books they start.

Will you be one of the few who not only finishes—but implements? If so, congratulations in advance. Once you master the skills, strategies, and systems in this book, you'll unlock the kind of breakthroughs, freedom, fulfillment, and next-level success you've been striving for your entire life.

By the time you reach the end, you won't just understand the 4C² Success Formula—you'll know how to apply it. If you do the exercises and implement them consistently, you can create meaningful, measurable results in the areas that matter most—often sooner than you expect. And it all starts now.

So let's dive in—and begin building your next-level success. This isn't theory—it's the real-world framework the most successful entrepreneurs are already using, whether they realize it or not. Some discovered it through decades of trial and error; others were fortunate enough to be mentored into it.

The **Entrepreneur 4C² Success Formula** is your shortcut—distilled, proven, and ready to execute. You no longer need to guess. You just need to implement what the world's top entrepreneurs already do.

CHAPTER 1

Are You Stuck in the Achievement Loop?

*"Your current life is the result of the
standards you've accepted."*

— TONY ROBBINS

You're doing everything "right"… so why does it still feel like something's missing?

If you saw yourself in my story, you already know the problem. You've set ambitious goals, shown up early, worked late, sacrificed weekends, and invested in coaching and books—and yes, it's produced results others admire. But does it feel the way you hoped? Are you free, or still waiting for life to match the picture in your head?

You're not failing—you're following a pattern that delivers progress without peace, results without joy. Success built at the expense of your life leads to one predictable outcome: regret.

You don't need more grit—you need a new game plan. It starts by naming the real issue and stepping out of the loop that's been running you.

Most entrepreneurs are trapped in what I call the *Achievement Loop*—and they don't even realize it. It's the model we've been handed from the start: a loop disguised as ambition, hustle, and drive—but one that silently leads to stress, isolation, and eventual burnout.

I remember waking up in the middle of the night, already running through my to-do list before the sun came up. My mind wouldn't switch off. I told myself this was the cost of success—just part of the process. I later learned I wasn't alone. Nearly 70% of entrepreneurs report sleep issues like insomnia or stress-related sleep interruptions.[1] For me, that statistic wasn't a number—it was my life. Maybe it's yours too.

And the pressure doesn't stop when the day begins. It follows you everywhere. You feel like you're always behind, always pushing to keep up. I saw it in the people around me too— friends, peers, colleagues—living in a constant state of urgency. No wonder 92% of small business owners say they feel stressed at least once a week, and 41% feel it every day.[2] If you are feeling that same relentless push, you are not alone.

That strain has a way of isolating you. I'd come home from long days with nothing left to give, convincing myself I was "doing it for them," yet feeling increasingly disconnected from the people I loved. Again, I discovered I wasn't alone—half of all entrepreneurs report feeling lonely on a regular basis.[3] Do you recognize that feeling too?

And it doesn't stop with loneliness. The longer you stay trapped in the loop, the more it erodes your mental health. I've had moments where the pressure felt like an invisible weight I couldn't shake—and it was no surprise to learn entrepreneurs are twice as likely to experience depression and three times more likely to struggle with substance abuse.[4] For some, the cost is even higher. Their success stories end too soon, with suicide rate among entrepreneurs nearly double those of the general population.[5]

If any of this feels close to home, know this: you're not alone—and nothing about you is broken.

Here's the gut punch: after all that sacrifice, the payoff isn't even guaranteed. You already know my story of bankruptcy, and I've met countless business owners who worked themselves to the bone only to end up with very little to show for it. Sadly, that is more the rule than the exception. Only 10–15% of entrepreneurs ever build enough financial security to retire comfortably.[6] Nearly one in five small business owners net less than $25,000 a year, and only about a third break the $100,000 mark.[7] If you have been grinding, but the numbers still don't add up, you're not imagining it.

Meanwhile, your relationships often pay the price. I've felt the strain in my own marriage and watched others lose the people they care about most. If your relationship has suffered under the weight of your ambitions, you're far from alone—entrepreneurs are 5–10% more likely to divorce than those in traditional jobs.[8]

These numbers aren't just statistics—they're warning lights. Signs that the system we've been told to follow was never designed to serve your life, only your output. Left unchecked, those warnings harden into regrets: the missed games, the strained marriage, the health challenges, the years you can't reclaim.

Most entrepreneurs are trapped in this pattern—the *Achievement Loop*, or the *A-Loop*, for short. It looks like the path to success. Society praises it. It's the narrative we've all inherited—and many of us have lived.

But here's the truth: what's sold as ambition, drive, and hustle can quietly become a trap. We glorify the grind—but rarely question its cost.

Entrepreneurs don't fail because they're lazy. They fail because they've been running on a broken map—a compass stuck on "next." No matter which way you turn, it keeps pulling you in the same direction.

From the start, we're taught the same formula: dream big, work harder, sacrifice more, and keep climbing until you "make it." It sounds noble. Admirable. But beneath the surface, it creates a loop that looks like progress while quietly draining your life.

Here's how it plays out:

Step 1: Set Big Goals

You're told to dream bigger than feels realistic. *"If your goals don't scare you, they're not big enough."*

At seventeen, I set my first huge goal: become a millionaire. I believed that number would fix everything—security, the dream house, freedom, peace. Maybe you've done the same. You tie everything you want in life to a single target, convinced that once you hit it, everything changes.

But the truth: the bigger the goal, the heavier the pressure—and the easier it becomes to ignore the cost along the way.

Step 2: Create a Why

Once the big goal is set, you're told to anchor it with a powerful "why." And not just any reason—it has to be so emotional that it *"makes you cry."* The message is clear: if your *why* is strong enough, nothing can stop you.

So you dig deep. You say it's for your family, your kids, your future. That's what I told myself too. I said it was for Kim and the life we'd one day build together. It sounded noble. It sounded selfless.

But here's the reality: a "why" like that can become a shield. It gives you a reason to push harder—but it also justifies sacrifice, stress, and endless hustle. You tell yourself it's worth it—because it's for them.

Step 3: Sacrifice

Then comes the mantra: *"Success requires sacrifice."* Miss the dinners. Skip the games. Trade the present for a future that's always "just around the corner."

Kim's family loved to get together—game nights, dinners, simple moments that built connection. But when she asked me to come, my answer was almost always the same: "Sorry, I have to work." I convinced myself it was temporary. That one day, after I hit the goal, we'd travel the world together and make it up.

But every *no* chipped away at what we already had. I thought I was building a future for us—when in reality, I was eroding the present.

Maybe you've told yourself the same story: *it's only for now.* But here's the truth—every sacrifice collects interest. And every "no" becomes a debt you can't repay later.

Step 4: Embrace the Suck

When the pressure builds, you're told to wear it like a badge of honor. *"Grind now, shine later."* Exhaustion isn't a warning sign—it's proof you're serious.

I wore my stress like armor. Long nights. Sleepless mornings. A constant sense of urgency. I told myself it was strength—that I could outwork, outlast, and out-suffer anyone.

But it wasn't strength—it was suppression. Every unspoken fear, every buried frustration, every quiet doubt—I shoved it down and called it "grit."

The cost was real. It showed up in my health. In my mind. In my marriage. Yet instead of slowing down, I pushed harder—because that's what the loop tells you to do.

Step 5: Do Whatever It Takes

"Winners don't quit. Ever." That's the mantra. If you're serious, you go all in. No hobbies. No distractions. No excuses.

So you start cutting. First the hobbies. Then the downtime. Then the simple joys that once made life feel alive. For me, it was golf. I loved it. But eventually I gave it up, convincing myself real estate was my hobby now—that I didn't need anything else.

The truth? I felt guilty for enjoying anything that didn't move me closer to my goal. Fun became a liability. Rest felt irresponsible. And joy—joy became something I postponed, always promising I'd get back to it "someday."

Step 6: Achieve the Goal

You're taught that when you finally "make it," everything changes. That milestone—the million dollars, the business, the dream house—was supposed to be the gateway to freedom, peace, and happiness.

For me, that moment came twenty-three years later. We were millionaires on paper. But nothing changed. No joy. No magic. Just emptiness.

Here's the truth: every achievement only proves that the goalpost doesn't deliver what you thought it would. Fulfillment wasn't waiting at the top. It wasn't even on the map. And that's where the real trap begins.

Step 7: Never Be Satisfied

The loop teaches one final rule: never be satisfied. No matter what you've built, it's never enough. So you reset the game—back to Step 1: Set bigger goals, invent another 'why,' sacrifice more, grind harder, achieve—and repeat. Faster. Harder. Louder.

So what did I do? I raised the bar. I was a millionaire, so now I had to be a multi-millionaire. I started more companies—title, lending, handyman services—each one I sold myself (and Kim) on as "the thing" that would finally make it all worth it.

In reality, I was just restarting the loop.

That's the trap: Step 7 isn't an ending—it's a reset button. Round and round it goes. Unless you change the formula, you don't break free. You don't arrive—you just loop.

The loop doesn't end when you succeed. It ends when you wake up.

I know this loop because I lived it—for 27 years. And I'm not the exception; I'm the rule. Most entrepreneurs follow this exact path. And for most, it doesn't end in success—it ends in burnout, broken relationships, failing health, and starting over from scratch.

If any of this feels familiar, you're already in the loop.

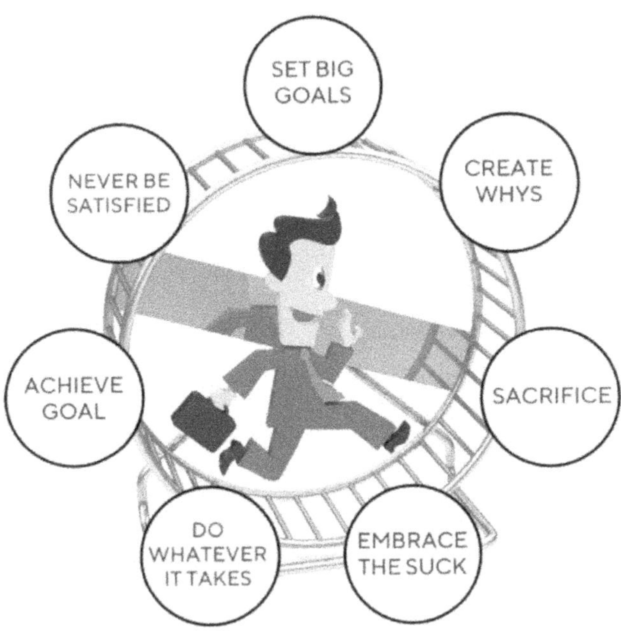

And if you're in it right now—it's not your fault. You've been following a map that was never meant to lead you home. This is what we were taught. This is what society rewards. This is the blueprint we were handed.

But the loop doesn't lead to fulfillment—it leads to burnout. And the worst part? Most people don't even realize they're in it until it's already stolen years of their life—or quietly fractured the relationships they care about most.

The danger of the Achievement Loop isn't that it looks like failure. The danger is that it looks like the *right* way to live. That's why so many smart, driven entrepreneurs wake up with impressive résumés—and lingering regrets.

Society praises people caught in it. We call them hustlers, grinders, high performers. And the moment we pause, slow down, or question the loop… we feel guilty. Lazy. Like we're falling behind.

But here's the truth most won't admit:

- You can be winning in business—and still losing in life.
- You can hit every goal—and still feel something's missing.
- You can be productive—and still be stuck.
- You can be achieving—and still be unfulfilled.

If you've lived like that for years, it's not your fault. It's the system. The loop convinces us that success requires pain, that joy must be postponed, and that rest is weakness. But that's not success—it's survival. It teaches us to trade the present for a future that never truly arrives.

But what if you could build both—the dream and the day-to-day joy? What if you didn't have to lose yourself to succeed?

Even after my life collapsed—financially, emotionally, and relationally—and I made the decision to rebuild everything differently, I kept slipping back into the loop. The need to grind. The fear of slowing down. The pressure to always do more. It lingered—because that *Achievement Loop* was all I had ever known.

Then something shifted. I realized I didn't need more effort—I needed a better formula. I had already sacrificed everything once and ended up broke, burned out, and broken. I wasn't going to do that again. I needed a new way—not just to succeed in business and financially, but to succeed in life. A path that produced extraordinary results—and left me with no regrets.

That's when I began studying what the most successful entrepreneurs were doing differently. From that, I built the 4C² Success Formula—to make it simple, teachable, and repeatable.

Reflection Exercise: Your Loop Inventory

Before you move on, pause for a moment. Look at your own life through the lens of the loop.

- What's the biggest goal you're chasing right now?

- Why does it matter to you—really? Is it about freedom, or proving something?

- What have you been sacrificing along the way—time, health, connection?

- When you wake up each day, what emotions show up most often—joy, urgency, peace, pressure?

- Think back to your last big win. How long did the satisfaction last before you were chasing the next one?

- If nothing changed over the next five years, what would you regret most?

Take at least ten minutes here. Write down your answers. Be brutally honest. This clarity will set your mind for what's about to come.

Now ask yourself the most important question of all: *Is this the life I want to keep repeating—Or is it time for something better?*

If you're ready to step out of the Achievement Loop and into a life you won't regret, turn the page. In the next chapter, I'll walk you through the **Entrepreneur 4C² Success Formula**—a clear, repeatable framework drawn from what the most successful do differently. You will get the system and the tools; you'll decide where to apply them and how far to take them.

Whether your next level is:

- Scaling your business without burnout

- Creating financial freedom

- Rebuilding your marriage

- Renewing your health

- Feeling free again

…the same framework applies. If you do the exercises and implement consistently, you will create real progress in the areas that matter most.

And when you align your life with this formula, something shifts. Apply it consistently, and you stop chasing results—and start creating them. You stop sacrificing what matters—and start living.

The goal isn't just bigger wins—it's fewer regrets.

So if you're ready to stop spinning, start rising, and build a life you actually love—turn the page.

Your next-level success begins here.

How the Top 10% Achieve Extraordinary Results

"Success is not about working harder. It's about working smarter on the right things."

— Unknown

How many of your biggest wins have truly felt the way you imagined? You hit the milestone, celebrate for a moment… and the feeling fades.

The real question isn't whether achievement feels good—it's why it doesn't last. The goalpost keeps moving, the bar resets, and the loop continues. The Achievement Loop can deliver results—sometimes impressive ones—but often at the cost of your time, energy, and peace.

This chapter is about what the top 10% of entrepreneurs do differently—how they achieve results that stick and build lives that rise alongside them.

Because success without a life isn't success.

The Entrepreneur 4C² Success Formula is a smarter process built for a deeper kind of success—not just in business, but in every area that truly matters.

It's a framework created from observing what the top 10% of entrepreneurs actually do—those rare individuals who are not just wealthy, but fulfilled. Not just productive, but present. Not just admired, but fully alive.

They don't trade their life for success

They build success around the life they actually want.

And now, you can too.

The 4C² Success Formula isn't theory. It's a proven, teachable, and repeatable framework designed to help you create extraordinary results—faster, with greater joy, and without losing yourself in the process.

Where the Formula Came From

When I decided to rebuild my life, I didn't want to climb back on the hamster wheel—just with a shinier treadmill this time. I wanted to understand what the top 10% of *truly* successful entrepreneurs were doing differently. Not the ones with the biggest companies or the flashiest social media profiles—the ones who were actually happy. Fulfilled. Free.

At first, I did what most people do: I studied the big names—the wealthy, the well-known, the ones everyone seemed to admire. But the deeper I looked, the more I saw something most people miss.

It was like booking a dream vacation after seeing breathtaking photos online—only to arrive and find the beach covered in seaweed, the water murky, and the hotel under construction. On the brochure, it looked perfect. In reality, it was nothing like what was promised.

That's what I found when I looked past the glossy public images of many I once admired.

On the surface, they had million-dollar launches, luxury homes, and enviable lifestyles. But behind the curtain, the very pursuit of those achievements had taken a toll—sometimes one they would later regret.

Take **Mohamed El-Erian**, former CEO of investment giant PIMCO. By every measure, he was one of the most successful people in the world. Yet one day, his young daughter handed him a list of 22 milestones he had missed—everything from her first soccer game to her first day of school. In his own words, it made him realize his "work-life balance had gotten way out of whack."[9] That relentless pursuit of professional achievement had cost him moments he could never get back.

Or consider **Arianna Huffington**. While running *The Huffington Post*, one of the most influential media companies on the planet, she collapsed from exhaustion—hitting her head on her desk and breaking her cheekbone. "I had bought into the collective delusion that burnout is the price we must pay for success,"[10] she later admitted. Her body had literally given out because the Achievement Loop demanded more than it could sustain.

And it wasn't just icons. Everyday entrepreneurs told the same story.

Mary, an agency founder with a solid book of business, hit all her targets yet carried a quiet guilt for the moments she missed—with her kids, her husband, her life.

Jack, a regional contractor with a full backlog, looked back at his calendar and saw no memories—no weekends away, no laughter, no living. Just twelve months of work that never felt like living.

These stories are powerful reminders: **extraordinary results mean little if they cost us what matters most.**

These are only four examples—yet I saw the pattern almost everywhere. On the outside, they seemed to have it all. But on the inside, their lives were quietly unraveling. Many were on their third marriage—and that one was hanging by a thread. They barely knew their kids. Their health was in shambles. They looked successful… but they had sacrificed everything for it.

We've been trained to admire the outcome without questioning the path. That's not sustainable success—it's survival disguised as achievement.

And the worst part? That's what most of us are chasing. We mimic their version of success—their habits, their hustle, their systems—but we rarely stop to ask: **Is that the life I actually want?**

Once I stopped chasing the illusions and started studying entrepreneurs who were *genuinely* fulfilled, a new pattern emerged.

The top 10% play the game differently. They don't just chase wins—they build lives they can look back on with no regrets.

One was a small business owner I met at a mastermind. She wasn't famous, didn't have a big team, or a flashy brand. But what she had was rare: a thriving business that grew steadily year after year—with healthy margins, loyal clients, and real momentum.

Even more striking was how she lived. She wasn't glued to her business 24/7. Her schedule left room for family and for herself. She picked her kids up from school. She took weekends off, even Fridays too sometimes. She wasn't chasing clients; they were chasing her.

She didn't just build a business—she'd built a life she didn't need to escape from.

Her business was growing. Her income was rising. And her life was getting better, not more chaotic.

At the same event, I met another entrepreneur. His business was smaller than hers, and his income was half of what she made. But he looked exhausted. He'd missed his daughter's last two birthdays. He hadn't taken a real day off in over a year. And even though he was working 60+ hours a week, he still felt behind—constantly putting out fires, constantly chasing.

That moment was eye-opening. She was earning more, working less, and living better. He was grinding harder… and getting less.

It became clear: success isn't about how many hours you work—or how big your business is. It's about how aligned it is with what you truly want.

Alignment isn't a luxury—it's the ultimate leverage point.

Every high-performing entrepreneur I studied had it. They weren't sacrificing everything to succeed. They weren't hustling 24/7. They weren't burned out or broken. They were living aligned—intentional lives built around clarity, focus, and the right support.

After seeing the same patterns repeat —across industries, ages, and backgrounds—it became impossible to ignore. Each one of them was playing a different game. They weren't following the traditional rules of success; they were rewriting them. And they were winning because of it.

Despite their differences, they all shared five key characteristics. The first formed their foundation. The other four became the core elements—together forming what I call the *Entrepreneur 4C² Success Formula.*

You might be wondering why it's called the 4C² Success Formula. The 4C² represents four core elements—and within each, two key principles that both start with the letter C. That's what the "squared" (C²) represents: not math, but two C's in every element.

It's a formula designed to help entrepreneurs align, grow, and thrive—in business *and* in life. **It's not about doing more; it's about doing what matters most.** Once you understand it, you'll see why the most successful aren't working harder— they're working differently.

Each element is powerful on its own. But when you align all four on top of the foundation, something transformational happens. You unlock what I call next-level success—a life where your business grows, your relationships thrive, your health improves, and you feel deeply fulfilled—all at once, if you choose.

This isn't about balance—it's about alignment.

Next-level success also means you're not just achieving more— you're *experiencing* more. More freedom. More energy. More joy. More meaning. You're not hustling for the next win— you're building a life that feels like a win every day.

Success isn't a finish line—it's a lifestyle. And the beauty of this formula is its adaptability-wherever you apply it, it works.

You can use the 4C² Formula to:

- **Scale your business sustainably**
- **Achieve financial freedom**
- **Improve your health**
- **Rebuild your marriage**
- **Become a more present parent**
- **Achieve peace of mind**

Whatever your next level is—**this formula gets you there.**

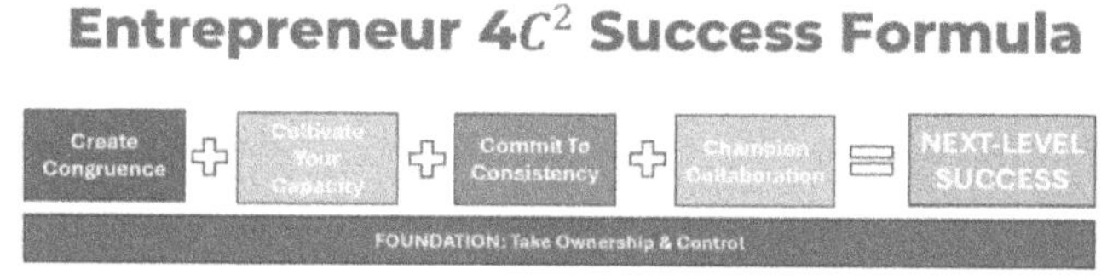

Here's a Brief Overview:

The Foundation You Can't Skip

If you look at the diagram above, you'll notice a solid base beneath the four core elements. That's not just design—it's the foundation that holds the entire Entrepreneur 4C² Success Formula together: **Take Ownership & Control.**

This is the first shift every successful entrepreneur makes. Without it, even the best strategies fall apart. If you don't fully own your time, energy, focus, and results, then by default, something—or someone—else will.

Ownership is what gives you back control. Without it, the entire structure collapses. Until you make this shift, you'll stay stuck in the Achievement Loop—reacting instead of leading, chasing instead of creating. But once you take full responsibility for how you show up, everything begins to change.

This mindset is what makes the rest of the formula work. You can't create congruence, build capacity, stay consistent, or collaborate effectively if you're constantly running on fumes, distracted, or living by default.

That's why the next chapter dives deeper into this principle—because it's not just a nice idea. It's the foundation that supports every breakthrough you want to create.

With **Ownership & Control** in place, the rest of the formula can finally stick. Here are the four core elements:

- **Create Congruence**—Align who you are with what you do. When you live out of sync, even big wins feel hollow.

- **Cultivate Your Capacity**—Expand what you're capable of so your business—and life—can expand with you.

- **Commit to Consistency**—Build rhythms and systems that make the right actions repeatable. That's how progress compounds.

- **Champion Collaboration**—Leverage people, partnerships, and support. You go farther, faster—and with less strain.

Why All Four Matter

You can grind like crazy and still get only a fraction of the payoff. But when all four elements align, everything changes.

Picture a four-reel slot machine. Each reel is one element—Congruence, Capacity, Consistency, Collaboration—and each area of your life is its own machine: business, health, marriage, money.

Most entrepreneurs already have one or two reels aligned. That's why they get line-pays: a strong quarter, a burst of energy, a few better nights at home. Real wins—then it fades. And they keep yanking the lever because the Achievement Loop tells them to: work harder, push longer, add another tactic—"one more launch, one more deal, one more 5 a.m."—and someday the jackpot will hit.

But that's playing odds, not building outcomes. The costs pile up while the missing reels never set.

The difference with the most successful entrepreneurs? They don't play odds—they take control. The foundation—**Take Ownership & Control**—flips the machine from *chance* to *set-mode*. From there, they align the reels—**Congruence, Capacity, Consistency, Collaboration**—until the pattern locks.

That's when the jackpot—the freedom and fulfillment you actually want—triggers by design, not luck.

You don't do this once; you do it one machine at a time. The good news? You're probably just one or two reels away. This formula shows you how to set the rest on purpose—so you can stop spinning and start winning.

Ask yourself:

- Where are two or three reels already aligned?

- Which reel is missing—and are you still pulling the lever, hoping it lands?

- What opens up when you flip the switch and align all four in one area first?

That's what I discovered. And that's what the top 10% already know—whether they call it this or not.

Here's what makes the $4C^2$ Success Formula different: it doesn't just create results—it creates *aligned* results. It doesn't take years—when implemented fully, change starts sooner than you expect. And it doesn't demand harder work—it helps you work smarter, live better, and grow faster.

Let me give you a simple example.

Imagine two people trying to get to New York City. The first decides to walk. He's committed. He's disciplined. He's proud of how hard he's working. He starts early, pushes through exhaustion, and keeps telling himself that if he just works harder, he'll eventually get there.

And he does. But it takes months. By the time he arrives, he's burned out, worn down, and too drained to enjoy the destination he fought so hard to reach.

The second person books a flight. Same destination—completely different journey. They arrive faster, with more energy, and ready for what's next—without destroying themselves along the way.

In the end, the real win isn't proving how hard you can push—it's reaching your destination with the energy, freedom, and clarity to enjoy what you've built… and to keep building without burning out.

That's the difference between chasing success with sheer effort and creating it through the right formula. The first drains everything from you; the second gives it all back.

The **Entrepreneur 4C² Success Formula** is the flight—it gets you there faster, with less pain, and far more possibility.

Reflection Break:

- Where in your life or business are you still walking—pushing with sheer effort—when a better formula could help you fly?

- Where are you working harder than you need to, simply because you've never seen another way?

Pause here for five minutes. Write your answers. Don't just think—write.

This isn't about fitting into someone else's version of success. It's about defining what success actually means to *you*—and having the tools, structure, and support to create it. So you don't just succeed—you succeed on your terms, with a life that feels as good as it looks.

True success isn't borrowed—it's built.

Wherever you want change, wherever you want growth—**this is the formula to unlock it.**

Whether it's:

- More freedom
- More income
- More peace
- More connection
- More purpose

…the **4C² Success Formula** is the process that gets you there—faster than you think.

At its core, this formula is about creating a business and life you love—one you can look back on with pride, fulfillment, and no regrets.

You've just learned the 4C² Success Formula—the system the top 10% use to achieve extraordinary results.

But before you can apply it, there's something we need to address. Something most entrepreneurs spend their entire careers avoiding.

It's the reason smart entrepreneurs stay stuck. Why driven leaders burn out. Why your business grows while your life shrinks.

In the next chapter, I'm going to tell you what it is—and it won't be comfortable.

Your first instinct will be to resist it. To rationalize it. To explain why it doesn't apply to you.

But every entrepreneur who's built real freedom—the kind that includes health, relationships, and peace—started by accepting one radical truth.

Actually, five truths. Five hard truths most entrepreneurs avoid because they require letting go of blame, putting yourself first when you've been taught that's selfish, and redesigning your business instead of just grinding harder.

I avoided them for 27 years. It cost me everything. When I finally faced them, everything changed.

Here's the radical truth: the entire 4C² Success Formula is built on a foundation—Take Ownership & Control. Without it, the rest collapses.

And that foundation starts with five truths you must accept.

Are you ready?

Turn the page.

Before You Keep Reading… Take the Success Diagnostic

You've just met the Entrepreneur $4C^2$ Success Formula. Take 4–7 minutes to see where you stand. The online Entrepreneur Success Diagnostic reveals your current zone—Danger, Momentum, or Power—for each of the five components and gives you a clear snapshot of your strengths and gaps. Results are instant. Knowing your baseline now will make everything that follows hit even harder.

Take it now: https://www.MySuccessDiagnostic.com

Prefer to stay offline? Flip to the print-friendly Entrepreneur Success Diagnostic in the Appendix.

CHAPTER 3

The Radical Truth Most Entrepreneurs Avoid

(And Why It's the Key to Everything)

"Real success is about creating a life that incorporates financial abundance and personal fulfillment. Make your goal to be wealthy in all aspects of life—financially, mentally, emotionally, and spiritually."

— DAYMOND JOHN

You built the life you have right now. All of it.

The business that's thriving or struggling. The marriage that's connected or distant. The body that's strong or breaking down. The bank account that's growing or stagnant.

You created it—through your choices, your actions, your patterns, and yes, your avoidance.

I warned you in the introduction: this book isn't here to tell you what you want to hear. And this is one of those moments.

Change doesn't begin with action—it begins with ownership.

Here's the Radical Truth Most Entrepreneurs Avoid—Actually, It's Five Truths:

Truth #1: You created the life you have right now. Not the economy. Not your team. Not your spouse. Not bad luck. You. Through every choice you made, every pattern you followed, every action you took—and every action you didn't take.

Truth #2: If you created it, you can change it. That's not a burden—it's your greatest power. If your choices built your current reality, new choices can build a different one.

Truth #3: But change only happens when you put yourself first. Not your business. Not your clients. Not everyone else's demands. Your energy, your time, your priorities—they must come before the world's expectations.

Truth #4: Your business exists to serve your life, not consume it. If it's running you instead of you running it, the formula is backwards. Most entrepreneurs build a prison and call it success.

Truth #5: None of this works until you stop living reactively. Stop letting your phone, your inbox, and other people's urgencies dictate your day. Proactive living isn't a luxury—it's the only way forward.

Most entrepreneurs will never accept these truths. They're too hard. Too confronting. Too different from everything they've been taught about hustle and sacrifice.

They'll resist. They'll rationalize. They'll explain why their situation is different.

But every entrepreneur who's built real success—the kind that includes freedom, health, relationships, and joy—started by accepting all five.

Here's why this is the key to everything: Without these truths active in your life, the **4C² Success Formula** can't work. You can have perfect congruence, strong capacity, consistent systems, and great collaborators—but if you're not in control, it all collapses.

That's why the entire formula is built on a single foundation: **Take Ownership & Control.**

Entrepreneur $4C^2$ Success Formula

As you can see, the four core elements don't float on their own—they rest on a solid base. This is the bedrock that makes everything else work. Without full ownership of your time, energy, mindset, and choices—and without reclaiming control of your schedule and direction—the rest of the formula won't hold. This is the ground everything else stands on. Miss it, and nothing works long term. Master it, and everything accelerates.

This foundation has two parts that work together:

First, you must take ownership. That means accepting that you created your current reality—through your choices, actions, and patterns. No blame. No excuses. Just ruthless responsibility for what is.

Second, you must take control. That means using that ownership to seize authority over what happens next—your time, your energy, your business design, and your daily priorities.

You can't take control until you take ownership. And ownership without control leaves you stuck—accepting reality but powerless to change it. Both are required.

So let's start with taking full ownership—not just of your business, but of your energy, time, relationships, and health—and then learn how to take control through two of the most important shifts most entrepreneurs never make: living a **'You First' Life** and choosing to **live proactively,** not reactively.

These shifts aren't suggestions—they're requirements. Without them, the formula fails. Without ownership, nothing changes. Without a 'You First' life, nothing aligns. And without a proactive mindset, order gives way to chaos.

You can't master your business until you master yourself.

The true cost of avoiding ownership isn't just slower progress—it's looking back and realizing you sacrificed the moments and priorities that mattered most. Ownership is how you build a business and a life you can look back on with pride—and no regrets.

Truth #1 & #2: You Created This—And You Can Change It

It doesn't matter how uncomfortable this feels. If you want change, you must face it: you are exactly where your patterns have placed you.

There are rare exceptions—injury, chronic illness, systemic shocks—but in every other case, your current reality reflects the compound effect of your actions, decisions, and habits, along with your inaction.

If your business isn't working, it's not your team, the economy, or "the market." You hired the team. You picked the market. You choose how to respond to the economy.

If your marriage is struggling, own your part—how you show up, listen, and repair.

If your health is slipping, it's the choices you make every day.

That might be hard to hear, but it's also the most empowering truth you'll ever accept. If you're part of the cause, you can be the cause of the change. If you created it, you can change it. That's the most powerful truth you'll ever own.

The most successful entrepreneurs share one thing: ruthless ownership. No blame. No excuses. Just responsibility. When you own everything within your control, you can transform almost anything that matters.

Let's be direct: if you don't take ownership, everything else in this book will eventually collapse—like a house without a foundation. No strategy survives long on a foundation of excuses.

Truth #3: You Must Put Yourself First

Ownership is the foundation—but it's not enough on its own. Once you own your outcomes, the next question becomes: what kind of life do you want to build from here?

Most entrepreneurs answer with strategy, hustle, or sacrifice. But if you want next-level success—the kind that lasts—you must embrace a deeper truth: you must start with you. You must live a 'You First' life.

You are the common denominator in every area of your life. Upgrade yourself, and everything rises.

Most entrepreneurs don't. Too often, they sacrifice health, peace, relationships, and joy in service of "the hustle." It can feel noble—even responsible—to put yourself last, but it's a fast path to burnout.

Chronic self-sacrifice erodes the very things your success depends on: the quality of your decisions, your energy, your leadership, your results. Think about the days you're exhausted and short-tempered—what kind of business decisions do you make then? What kind of partner or parent are you when you walk through the door depleted and distracted? What kind of leader are you when you're running on fumes? That isn't commitment—it's collapse disguised as duty.

Now flip the script. When you're rested, focused, energized, and present, you make cleaner decisions, lead with clarity, and show up as your best—not your leftovers. The work improves, the wins compound, and both your team and your family feel the difference. That version of you wins. That version creates next-level success—in every area of life.

One entrepreneur I worked with used to wake up at 5 a.m., go nonstop all day, and still felt like she wasn't doing enough. Her health was declining. Her marriage was strained. Her team was burning out too. When she finally committed to a 'You First' Life, everything changed. She protected her mornings. Delegated with clarity. Took weekends off. Her revenue didn't drop—it grew. More importantly, she did too. When she stopped sacrificing herself, everything around her began to thrive. She didn't just get her time back. She got herself back.

Here's the truth most people miss: living a 'You First' Life isn't about rest or rituals—it's about reclaiming control in a world designed to keep you reacting.

Today's world is built to hijack your attention. Tech companies spend billions engineering apps to keep you scrolling, tapping, and checking. Your phone buzzes. A notification flashes. A new crisis pops up—and before you know it, your life is no longer your own.

Most entrepreneurs live in reaction mode—answering emails, responding to texts, tackling urgent tasks, jumping from meeting to meeting—never fully in control of their focus, time, or energy. It's a cycle of exhaustion that feels productive but keeps you stuck. Busyness masquerades as progress—until you realize you're running in circles.

To live a 'You First' Life, you must also choose to live a Proactive Life. A Proactive Life means you lead your day—your day doesn't lead you. It means setting your own priorities instead of reacting to everyone else's. It means protecting your time, energy, and focus—like your success depends on it. Because it does.

And while dozens of distractions try to pull you back into reaction mode each day, two sabotage entrepreneurs the most:

1. **Their business**—always begging for your attention at all hours

2. **Their phone**—a constant stream of noise, distraction, and other people's agendas

Taking control of your life means mastering these two forces— or they will master you. Left unchecked, they'll drain your focus and dictate the direction of your day.

But before we tackle those challenges, let's bust the biggest lie entrepreneurs believe: "Taking care of myself first is selfish."

It's actually the opposite of selfish. When you're exhausted, distracted, and disconnected, your family, your team, your clients, and your mission all suffer. When you're running on empty, everyone around you feels it.

'You First' doesn't mean only you. It means starting with you—so the world gets the best of you, not what's left of you. Just like they announce on every flight: put your oxygen mask on first. If you can't breathe, you can't help anyone else.

You must take care of yourself first—so that you are capable of taking care of everything else in your business and life.

What a 'You First' Life Actually Looks Like

You wake up energized—not already behind. You start your day on your terms, not the world's. You make decisions with clarity, not pressure. You spend time with your family and feel present, not distracted. You build your business around your life—not the other way around.

This isn't fantasy. It's the natural result of taking ownership and finally putting yourself first. Prioritizing your health, rest, mental clarity, and joy is how you maximize your contribution. It's how you make better decisions. It's how you lead—and live—at your highest level.

Most entrepreneurs believe that working 24/7 is the fastest path to success. But those who rest, protect their energy, and live intentionally often grow their businesses faster than those who grind themselves into the ground.

It's no different from fitness. Train every day without rest, and your body breaks down. Train, recover, and fuel properly, and your body grows faster and stronger. Your business, your mind, your results—they all work the same way. Sustainable effort always beats short bursts of burnout.

'You First' isn't just healthier—it's more effective. It's how you create next-level success faster. And once you take ownership of yourself—your time, your energy, your emotions—it's time to extend that ownership outward.

Truth #4: Your Business Should Serve You—Not the Other Way Around

If you want to live a 'You First' Life, you must take control of the single biggest drain on your energy: your business.

Here's a hard truth: most entrepreneurs are not running their business—their business is running them. They spend their days reacting—answering calls, putting out fires, staying "available," and sacrificing their lives in the name of growth.

But pause for a moment and ask yourself: why did you start your business in the first place?

Every entrepreneur's reason falls into one of three categories:

1. **To Change the World**—like Elon Musk or Jeff Bezos, driven by a massive global mission. This level of impact demands total sacrifice and tunnel vision. It's rare, and if that's you, be ready to dedicate everything—much like an Olympic athlete chasing gold. But if you are reading this book, you probably don't fall into this category.

2. **To Do What You Love**—you love your work so much you'd do it for free, even with a billion dollars in the bank. If that's true, amazing. But again, that's a small fraction of entrepreneurs—and likely not why you're here.

3. **To Create Freedom**—this is where 99% of entrepreneurs fall. They started their business to create time freedom, financial freedom, a lifestyle they love—to work with who they want, when they want, and how they want.

So here's the question: if your business exists to create freedom and serve you… *is it?*

Or are you serving it?

Let me tell you about Nels and Kim. They're chiropractors—and for years, they did what most entrepreneurs are taught to do: grind. They built a thriving practice with a full patient load, a big team, and steady income. But they were working 65+ hours a week, six or seven days a week. Constantly giving to others. Constantly putting themselves last. And it was slowly draining them.

They were taking care of everyone—except themselves. They were respected, busy, "successful." Yet behind the surface, they were burned out, disconnected, and quietly unhappy. Then everything changed.

They stopped and asked the question most entrepreneurs never ask: *"What kind of life do we actually want to live?"* By answering honestly, they realized they didn't just want more time off—they wanted control. They wanted to build a business that served them, instead of one that constantly demanded everything from them.

So they did. They sold their original practice, opened a smaller one closer to home, and set a bold intention: "We're only going to work 25 hours a week. Four days. That's it." And that's exactly what they did.

Within 12 months, they were earning the same net profit they'd once made working 65+ hours a week. Within 24 months, they were making 30% more—still only working 25 hours a week.

But the real win wasn't financial. They got their life back. They prioritized their health. They deepened their relationship. They made space for hobbies they'd neglected for years. Nels became a scratch golfer. Kim became—and still is—a professionally ranked cowboy mounted shooter.

They didn't get lucky. They got intentional. They chose to live a *You First* Life. They designed a business that supported their vision—instead of sacrificing their life to support the business. They chose success they could enjoy now and look back on years later with no regrets.

Maybe your version of freedom doesn't look like 25 hours a week. Maybe it's more travel, never missing your kid's game, or simply having the energy to enjoy the life you've built. The details differ, but the principle is the same: your business should serve you.

You get to design a business around what matters most—whatever that looks like for you. Some entrepreneurs we work with don't want fewer hours at all. They're driven to grow faster, earn more, or build something bigger—but without burning out, sacrificing their health, or feeling like life is on hold. They're not looking to slow down. They're just done grinding the wrong way.

Whether you want more time, more freedom, or more financial growth without working longer hours, it all starts the same way: taking full ownership, living a You First Life, and building success around what truly matters to you.

Because if your freedom is gone, your business has lost its purpose. If your schedule, energy, and peace are dictated by your business, you're not in control. And if you're not in control of your business—you're not in control of your life.

Truth #5: Stop Living Reactively—Take Back Control of Your Time

Your phone is the second biggest thief of your time, attention, and energy—and most entrepreneurs don't even realize it. If your business pulls you into reaction mode, your phone is its most loyal accomplice.

It was designed to make you more productive, more connected, and more efficient. But left unchecked, it does the opposite. It hijacks your focus, drains your energy, and fractures your day into a thousand distractions—all while convincing you that you're "on top of things."

The problem isn't the phone itself—it's how you use it. A phone used proactively looks very different: you control when you check it. You schedule time to return calls, texts, or DMs. You turn off notifications so they don't hijack your attention.

You don't look at it first thing in the morning—not until you've taken care of yourself first.

Most entrepreneurs grab their phone within five minutes of waking up. And instantly, their day belongs to someone else. A client's email. A team message. A breaking headline. A social media ping. Your mood, your mindset, your focus— all hijacked before you've even decided who you want to be that day.

Almost every entrepreneur I work with is shocked by how many hours they reclaim—and how quickly they feel back in control—after a simple phone reset. One client put it best: *"My mornings are mine again."*

If you want to live a 'You First' Life and achieve the kind of extraordinary results top performers do, you must treat your phone as the tool it's meant to be—not the master it's become. Set business hours—and honor them. Turn off default notifications. Give yourself space each morning before ever looking at your phone. And most importantly—train the world to follow your rules, not the other way around.

Here's the truth: if your phone controls your attention, it controls your life. Take back your phone, and you take back your freedom.

Your "Take Control" Challenge

It's time to take control of your life and business. Not someday. Not "when things calm down." Now.

1. Decide That YOU Are In Control

Make the decision. Say it out loud. Write it down right now. From this point forward: your business exists to serve your life—not the other way around. You are the priority, not just a piece of the puzzle. This is the moment everything begins to shift—if you decide it does.

2. Schedule One Full Week Off—Right Now

Don't check your workload. Don't wait to "see how things go." Pick the week right now—any week in the next 12 months— then book it. Flights, hotel, deposit—whatever it takes. Do it before you turn this page. This one act will instantly reshape how you design your business and your life.

3. Plan Something Fun—In The Next 30 Days

Not productive, not strategic. Fun. Do something you've been putting off or ignoring. Pick the date right now and put it on your calendar. Joy is not a reward—it's a requirement for long-term success.

4. Set Your Ideal Working Hours—And Lock Them In

Decide your boundaries right now. Write them down. Then add them to your calendar as recurring blocks. Once you set the rules, everything else adjusts around them—just like Nels and Kim did.

Here's how I do it: I work from 11 a.m. to 6 p.m., Sunday through Thursday (sometimes Saturday). Before 11 a.m. is my time—non-negotiable. From 6–9 p.m., I'm fully with my wife and family. After that, since I'm a night owl, I'll often work another block from 9 p.m. to midnight. It's intentional, energizing, and it works for me.

That's not a prescription—it's proof. You don't have to follow "normal" hours, or what you think the business demands. Build the rhythm that fits your life—then protect it.

5. Set Boundaries With Your Phone—Starting Tomorrow Morning

Before you go to bed tonight, turn off all non-essential notifications. Tomorrow morning do not check your phone first thing. Instead, schedule two specific times each day to respond to messages, emails, and social media—then add those times to your calendar right now. You decide when and how you engage—not your phone.

None of this is about restriction—it's about reclaiming your power.

These aren't rules to follow. They're freedoms to fight for.

If these sound like a big shift—they are. But every next-level entrepreneur I've worked with had to make them. And every single one of them says the same thing afterwards: *"I wish I had done this sooner."*

Don't let years slip by before you realize the same truth. Take control now—because no one else will do it for you.

And here's the fastest way to lock it in: **reflect in writing.** Clarity doesn't come from more thinking—it comes from putting pen to paper.

Reflection Exercise: Own It and Design It

Grab a pen. Write this down. Don't just think it—capture it on paper. That's where clarity begins.

- Where in your life or business are you blaming others or circumstances?

- What results are you tolerating—and what would change if you owned them?

- Is your business serving you, or are you serving your business?

- What does your ideal 'You First' Life look like—in work, health, and relationships?

- What's one boundary you can implement this week to reclaim your power?

This isn't just about self-awareness. It's about anchoring the most important decision in your entrepreneurial journey: taking full ownership and control.

Ownership is not just a mindset shift—it's a line in the sand. It's the foundation that supports everything else you're about to build. Without it, the formula collapses. With it, every other part of the 4C² Success Formula comes alive—and your progress becomes unstoppable.

From this point forward, you're no longer at the mercy of your schedule, your stress, or other people's demands. You've taken back the driver's seat. You've chosen to lead. You've poured the foundation.

Now it's time to build the structure—and unlock the life you actually want.

Here's the radical truth: you've been the author all along. You created the results you have today—and you have the power to write what comes next.

Quick Reminder: Get Your Baseline

If you haven't taken the Entrepreneur Success Diagnostic yet, now's the time. In just 4–7 minutes, you'll get a clear snapshot of your current zone—Danger, Momentum, or Power—across all five components. You'll see exactly where you're strong, and where hidden gaps may be holding you back.

Start now: https://www.MySuccessDiagnostic.com

Or scan the QR code to begin.

Prefer paper? Use the print-friendly diagnostic in the Appendix.

Now that you've taken full ownership and control, chosen to live a 'You First' Life, and reclaimed authority over your business and phone, it's time to align the inside with the outside. Because if your identity, beliefs, and actions aren't in congruence with your goals, nothing else will hold.

Next, we move into the first core element of the 4C² Success Formula: *Create Congruence*. You've taken the wheel—now it's time to set the GPS to the exact destination you want.

If you've ever felt like you were working hard yet still out of sync, what comes next will bring clarity on an entirely new level.

So turn the page—it's time to align everything and build success that finally fits you.

CHAPTER 4

Are You Chasing the Wrong Goals?

(Element #1 Create Congruence)

*"Don't climb the ladder of success only to
realize it's leaning against the wrong wall."*

—STEPHEN COVEY

If your goals worked perfectly, would you actually want the
life they'd produce?

Most entrepreneurs don't fail from lack of targets or effort—
they fail because their targets aren't aligned with the life they
truly want. That's misalignment: achieving the numbers while
missing your life.

Top performers flip the script. They don't just chase goals—
they create congruence. Every target, milestone, and action
is designed to build toward the life they actually want to live.

Create Congruence is the first core element of the *Entrepreneur 4C² Success Formula* for a reason. It aligns your inner compass, your business, your goals, and your daily actions—so results compound in the right direction.

It's not just where we start—it's what makes everything else possible.

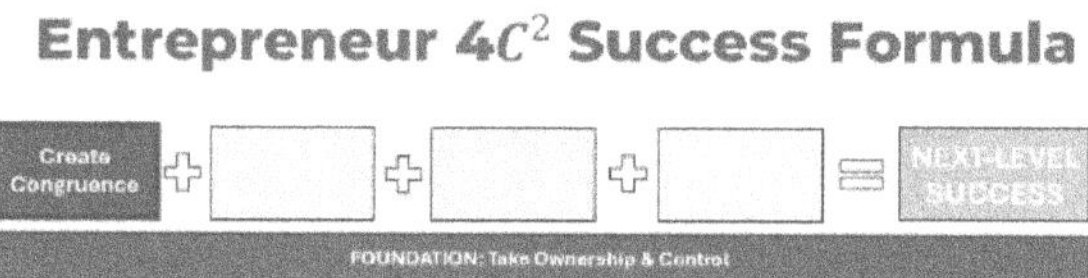

When your life and business are out of alignment, lasting momentum becomes impossible—no matter how hard you work.

Imagine buying a car because everyone insisted it was the best on the market—sleek, powerful, and packed with features. But every time you drive it, something feels off. You realize it's built for speed when what you wanted was comfort. You craved adventure, but it was designed for the track.

It looks great from the outside—but it's not built for *your* road.

That's what happens when you chase goals that don't align with your true vision. You might hit the milestones, but they won't take you where you actually want to go. Misalignment always erodes results, energy, and joy.

If your goals don't reflect what you truly want… if your daily actions don't bring you closer to your dream life… if your business pulls you away from your values… you'll feel resistance, stress, and misalignment—often without knowing why.

What Does It Mean to Create Congruence?

Congruence is alignment. It's when every part of your life and business works *together,* not against each other. When you're congruent, everything compounds. When you're not, everything collides.

Here's the real order of alignment:

- **Your Inner Compass**—your true vision. Not what looks good on paper. Not what others expect. But what you genuinely want, deep down.

- **Your Business**—it should support your Inner Compass and your vision, not pull you away from them.

- **Your Goals**—they should reflect your vision, not ego-driven checkboxes to impress others or grow for growth's sake. Your goals should point to how you want to live, not just what you want to earn.

- **Your Daily Actions**—What you actually do each day. A few non-negotiable habits, clear start-and-stop boundaries, and a quick check that today matched your Compass.

When these four components align, everything unlocks. You stop grinding and start flowing. You stop pushing and start progressing. You stop burning out and start lighting up. Alignment isn't a luxury—it's the ignition. It's what sparks momentum and keeps you moving in the right direction.

When you're congruent, drive comes naturally. You don't need to hype yourself up. You don't need external motivation. Think back to a time you fell in love or had a deep desire for something. You didn't need to write down your "why" every day. You didn't need accountability. You were *pulled* forward—because your actions matched your desires.

That's what happens when you live and work in alignment: you're no longer forcing progress; you're being pulled toward it. The entrepreneurs who achieve next-level success all share this edge: congruence.

You've probably been told to "find your why." But here's the truth most won't tell you: if your goals come from the wrong place, your "why" is fake—no matter how passionate it sounds.

A powerful "why" can't fix a misaligned "what."

An entrepreneur once told me his goal was to become a billionaire.

"Why?" I asked

"To push myself and leave a legacy."

I asked if that was truly his why—or something he'd absorbed. He was convinced it was real.

Six months later, he was diagnosed with prostate cancer. Fortunately, the surgery went well, and during recovery, he got honest with himself. What he actually wanted wasn't billions—it was freedom. Time with family and friends. Work he was proud of. A life he didn't miss while chasing it.

When he realigned his goals with that truth, everything changed. He laughed more. He felt lighter. He finally enjoyed his days. The drive was still there—but now it was aimed at what mattered most.

He's not the only one. On paper, a lot of goals sound noble. But underneath, many are about proving, pleasing, or keeping up. They often sound like this:

"I want to hit 7 figures to provide for my family." → Or is it really to prove you're good enough?

 "I want to build a team so I can scale my impact." → Or is it because you think that's what 'real' entrepreneurs do?

When your goals are born from ego, they'll always lead to exhaustion.

It's no different from health. Billions are spent convincing you that the number on the scale defines your worth. But that number says nothing about your energy, strength, or vitality. You can hit your "goal weight" and still feel weak, tired, and miserable.

Entrepreneurs do the same thing with revenue. They hit the target—and still feel empty. Achievement without alignment always feels hollow. That's what happens when you chase the wrong target: you get the outcome—but not the result you actually wanted.

When your goals are born from ego, fear, or comparison, the "why" you attach to them never feels real—and your motivation eventually fades.

Consider two entrepreneurs. Same industry. Same skill level.

Entrepreneur A sets a goal to scale to $10M because that's what "success" looks like. They build a business that consumes their time, drains their energy, and steals their joy. Even if they hit the number, they feel trapped by their own creation—stressed, burned out, and resentful.

Entrepreneur B flips the script. They start with vision—defining the life they want first: freedom, flexibility, fulfillment. Then they build the business to serve that life. Their offers, systems, and goals are designed to fit that design. The result? They're energized, focused, and in flow. Growth compounds naturally—and they often surpass $10M without sacrificing what matters most.

Same tactics, different sequence.

A starts with business goals and tries to retrofit life around them.

B starts with life constraints—hours, energy, values—and lets those constraints define the business: the goals, offers, calendar, and team.

That one shift changes every daily decision—what to sell, who to serve, what to decline—so the same effort compounds instead of getting wasted.

Who wins? The one with congruence.

Same industry. Same skills. Different peak.

A says yes to almost anyone. Stacks too many projects. Promises quick turnarounds. Stays "always on." Answers every ping immediately—so the calendar runs them.

B blocks life first—family, health, deep work—and builds the business inside those lines. Works only with clients they enjoy, takes fewer projects at once, sets clear hours and response times, and uses simple systems to protect those boundaries.

Same craft. Different rules. Different results.

How do you know you're on the wrong mountain?

- Every win buys more obligation, not more freedom.
- Revenue climbs while your **freedom metrics**—time, energy, presence—collapse.
- Your daily actions contradict your stated values.
- You keep saying, "After this next push…" for months—or years.

Success isn't about climbing the highest mountain; it's about climbing the *right* one.

Ironically, that's also how most people reach the highest peaks.

Most entrepreneurs are climbing a mountain that isn't theirs. Not by laziness—but by conditioning. It started with good intentions: goals that looked impressive, advice that sounded wise, mentors who meant well. They followed what seemed like the right path—until they realized it wasn't their path.

They reach the top and think: *"I didn't want this. I'm still not fulfilled. This isn't my dream."*

By then, the cost is clear—years, health, and relationships left behind.

Don't wait until the summit to realize you climbed the wrong peak. The real tragedy isn't just lost time—it's realizing you sacrificed years of energy for something you didn't even want.

That's why creating congruence now is so critical. It ensures you're climbing your mountain, not someone else's—so you can live, lead, and achieve with pride, fulfillment, and no regrets.

When we work with entrepreneurs, one of the first things we do is guide them through a powerful process to uncover their **Inner Compass**. It's an emotional and transformational experience that helps them reconnect with their true vision— and from that place, everything changes.

Decisions become easier. Drive feels natural. Goals reignite with meaning. The business starts working for them, not against them. When your vision is clear, your direction becomes automatic.

I once believed becoming a millionaire would give me what I truly wanted—security, peace, happiness, freedom. So I made it my identity. I chased it hard, sacrificing sleep, health, and time with loved ones, convinced the number would fix everything.

It didn't. The money brought success—but not satisfaction.

It was only through the 4C² Success Formula, that I finally understood. I had been doing everything right—setting big goals, finding emotional "whys," grinding like I was taught. But it all came from the wrong place: my ego, my conditioning, my idea of what success *should* look like.

And then it hit me:

I didn't want to be a millionaire. I wanted freedom.

The moment I made that simple shift—when I stopped chasing someone else's version of success and aligned everything with what I truly desired— everything changed.

That's why congruence hit me so deeply. I had lived the opposite for decades without realizing it. I was chasing money when what I really wanted was freedom.

What was amazing was that when I made that shift and started chasing the freedom, the money came faster and easier than when I was chasing the money.

Congruence doesn't just improve your direction—it transforms your results. When everything aligns, success compounds naturally—and often faster than you imagined.

But when it doesn't align, the cost creeps in quietly. Burnout doesn't announce itself. It shows up as a shorter fuse, strained patience, and constant fatigue. You keep pushing… until something breaks.

That's why alignment isn't optional. It's essential. That's the power of congruence—and the reason it's the first core element in the Entrepreneur 4C² Success Formula.

Your "Congruence" Reality Check

Imagine this: you've just been told you only have six months to live. No second chances. No do-overs.

Let that sink in.

Feel it fully before you continue—because only real emotion gives you real answers.

Now ask yourself:

- What would you stop doing immediately?
- Who would you spend time with?
- What would you prioritize?
- And most of all, how would you want to feel each day?

Next, zoom in on one area of your life—your business, your relationship, or your health.

Write down how you'd want it to *look* and *feel* if you only had six months left.

Be honest. Be bold. Be raw.

What you just wrote down isn't fantasy—it's your truth, stripped of filters. That's your Inner Compass. It's the life you actually want when fear, ego, and pressure fall away. When you live from this place, you don't just create success—you create a life you can look back on with peace, pride, and no regrets.

And here's the good news: you don't need a crisis to live this way. Clarity doesn't require a diagnosis—it requires **intention**.

Congruence is the ignition—but it's just the beginning. Once your vision is clear, the next question becomes: *do you have the capacity to drive it forward?*

Because no matter how aligned your goals are, you can't grow your business—or your life—beyond the skills and capacity you've built.

That's why the next step in the Entrepreneur 4C² Success Formula is **Cultivate Your Capacity.**

In the next chapter, you'll learn exactly how to expand it—and step into the version of yourself your vision demands.

Turn the page.

CHAPTER 5

What's Really Holding You Back?

(Element #2 Cultivate Your Capacity)

*"You don't become what you want.
You become what you believe."*

— OPRAH WINFREY

What if the only thing standing between you and your next level of success… is you?

That's not judgment—it's reality. Every high-performing entrepreneur eventually learns one truth: **your results will never outpace your growth.**

Your business won't scale beyond your capacity to grow.

Your relationships won't deepen beyond your capacity to connect.

Your freedom won't expand beyond your capacity to manage it.

Your results always rise—or fall—to the level of who you've become.

If you want extraordinary outcomes, you must first grow into the person capable of sustaining them. That's why the second core element of the Entrepreneur 4C² Success Formula is **Cultivate Your Capacity**—the process of expanding who you are to match what you're building.

Capacity isn't one thing—it's two kinds of skills working together. The first are **execution skills**; the second are **self-mastery skills**.

Execution skills are how you run the work—leading a team meeting with a clear agenda, crafting and finalizing a marketing plan, selling an offer and handling objections, presenting on a webinar or stage, negotiating terms, reading the P&L, assigning roles, and turning decisions into a simple plan people can follow. That's the *outer game*—the visible moves.

Self-mastery skills are how you run you. Saying no to a top client who wants to pull you into a 6 p.m. call that would steal family time. Refusing to let a harsh email dictate your mood. Walking into a tough conversation grounded and clear. Turning off your phone to stay focused. Moving forward despite self-doubt or outside noises. Making the hard, human call to let go of a loyal employee whose role has outgrown them. Closing the laptop at 5:30 because you promised time with the family. Protecting sleep, workouts, and thinking time as fiercely as revenue meetings—because that's what keeps you sharp.

Most entrepreneurs pour everything into execution skills—yet without self-mastery skills, those very skills can become the engine of burnout or self-sabotage.

I've seen it repeatedly: founders who've invested thousands of dollars into execution skills—courses, funnels, agencies—while investing almost nothing into self-mastery skills. Yet after 30–60 days of focused self-mastery in our work together, they see breakthroughs they'd been chasing for months or even years—without changing a single tactic.

You need both. Success isn't just about what you can do—it's about who you are when it matters most.

Here's the truth most entrepreneurs never hear: **you don't achieve goals—you grow into them.** When you grow into your goals, you're not just hitting targets; you're building a life and business you can look back on with pride and no regrets.

Your next level isn't earned through effort alone—it's unlocked through evolution.

You've probably said it before: "I don't have enough time." But is that really true? Or is it possible that time isn't the issue— skill is? What most people call a "time problem" is usually a *capacity problem* in disguise. Every entrepreneur gets the same 24 hours. The difference isn't how much time you have— it's what you're capable of doing with it.

Let's prove it. If a seasoned founder who's scaled three companies stepped into your business for 90 days, would results improve? Almost certainly. Not because they'd work more hours, but because they'd bring more capacity: clearer vision, tighter focus, better leadership, faster decisions. Same calendar, different output.

That's the point: the results you want are already possible. If you're not seeing them yet, it's not because you're incapable— it's because you haven't built the capacity required to create and sustain them.

And capacity isn't built on hours. It's built on two pillars: execution skills and self-mastery skills—the ability to perform at a high level under pressure and to stay grounded when things don't go your way.

You don't need more time. You don't need more hustle. You need to operate from a higher version of you.

And that's not a flaw. That's an invitation—a call to grow.

Think of a child in T-ball, dreaming of the Major Leagues. To get there, they must level up at every stage: Little League → High School → College → Minors → MLB. At each step, what's required? More skill. More growth. More development.

The two types of skills show up clearly here. **Execution skills—** hitting, speed, hand-eye coordination. But what separates a

Minor Leaguer from a Major Leaguer isn't execution alone—
it's **self-mastery**.

After 17 strikeouts in a row, one player steps up thinking, *"I'm due for a home run."* The other steps up afraid to strike out again. Same bat. Same swing. Different outcome.

By the time players reach the minors, their execution skills are nearly identical. What separates them is self-mastery.

And the same is true for entrepreneurs. You can't reach Major League goals with Little League skills. Without both execution and self-mastery skills, you stall. With both, you rise.

You see it all the time: an entrepreneur builds a million-dollar business, and everything seems to be working—until suddenly, it's not. Growth stalls. Problems multiply. Revenue plateaus.

So they scramble. New strategies. New hires. New systems. New offers. Nothing sticks. They might bump the ceiling a little, only to fall back. They regroup, push harder—only to bounce right back off the same invisible wall.

Most assume the problem is external: *"I need better systems." "I need a stronger team." "I need a new funnel."*

But the real issue? They've hit their **personal capacity ceiling**.

Your business can't rise above the version of you running it. Mindset, courage, and emotional resilience—those are what's maxed out. And just like the kid who can't move past Little League without new skills, your business can't grow past your current level of development.

It's like sprinting on a treadmill, convinced you're moving forward—while the ceiling presses down harder each time. You're moving, sweating, grinding… but staying stuck, wondering why the effort isn't turning into freedom.

The business isn't stuck. **You are**.

But here's the shift: once you turn inward—strengthening focus, boundaries, emotional resilience, courage, and energy—the ceiling disappears. Because you've grown into the person your next level requires.

That's the hidden ceiling almost no one talks about: the internal cap that stalls everything until you rise above it. That realization can sting—but it should also excite you. Because it means the solution is in your control.

You are not the problem. **You are the possibility**.

You're not stuck because of the market, your team, or the economy. You're stuck because the version of you running the show no longer matches the level you're trying to reach. The skills, habits, and mindset that got you here… can't get you there.

And now, it's time to upgrade.

Take Sarah, for example. She had a $1.2 million business that plateaued for three straight years. She kept chasing external fixes—consultants, team hires, new products—but nothing worked.

But the moment she turned inward—sharpening her focus, setting stronger boundaries, mastering her emotions—everything shifted. Within a year, her business grew to $2.6 million.

Same market. Same offer. **New version of her**.

The strategy didn't change—she did.

And that changed everything.

It wasn't just self-awareness. It was emotional control, mental discipline, and renewed execution. She wasn't just learning more—she was **becoming more**.

Still think you don't need to grow? Then answer these honestly:

- Have you hit a ceiling you can't seem to break through?
- Are you repeating patterns that used to work but no longer do?
- Are your old habits producing diminishing returns?

If you answered yes to any of these, capacity is the issue. And the solution? Your next breakthrough isn't out there—it's within.

So how do you expand it? You grow. You stretch. You upgrade the version of you running the show. And it starts with honoring how far you've already come. The skills that got you here are real achievements—you've built something others only dream of.

But if you're not yet living the life you truly want, it's because your current skillset has reached its ceiling. Let that sink in.

Breaking through your next level requires upgrading your capacity—not by adding more business tactics, but by developing higher-level self-mastery skills. These include mastering your mind, regulating your emotions, building courage, sustaining focus, being proactive, and generating energy. They're the hidden levers of exponential growth—and most entrepreneurs never develop them.

Why? Because they don't even know they exist. You can't train for a skill you've never been taught to value.

Even once you gain awareness, these skills don't strengthen themselves. Like physical muscles, they weaken when neglected—and the longer they're ignored, the harder they are to rebuild.

But, don't confuse self-mastery with execution skills. Execution skills are the external tactics—sales, marketing, messaging, presentations, hiring, leading meetings. Most entrepreneurs live here—and many are great at them. What they lack are the self-mastery skills that make execution consistent.

You don't need to replace your execution skills; you need to support them. Because without that foundation, tactical skills become inconsistent at best—and self-sabotaging at worst.

Think of it like this: execution skills are the gas pedal; self-mastery skills are the steering and brakes. Without both, you either stall out or crash.

There are many self-mastery skills to cultivate, but let's focus on three that shape everything—in business and in life.

Mind Mastery:

This is the ability to observe your thoughts instead of being ruled by them.

Imagine you're about to launch something new—a program, a partnership, an investment. Everything checks out on paper. Then the inner voice kicks in: *"What if I fail?" "Who am I to pull this off?" "I'm not ready."* And just like that, you freeze. You delay. You overthink. Not because it's the wrong move, but because your thoughts convinced you it was.

Most entrepreneurs don't fail because of bad ideas—they fail because they believed their bad thoughts.

Without mind mastery, your brain becomes the biggest barrier to your success. With it, you reclaim control. You still hear the doubt—but you act anyway. You question the story—instead of living inside it. That's the difference between sitting on a good idea for two years or launching it this month. Between spiraling into self-doubt or stepping into self-leadership.

The strongest minds don't silence fear; they simply stop obeying it. When you master your mind, the fear doesn't disappear—it just stops deciding your future.

Here's the real danger: without mind mastery, your business becomes hostage to your mindset. A bad day turns into a bad week. One comment crushes your confidence.

But when this skill is strong, you respond with clarity, not chaos—and that's what keeps you moving you forward. Without it, fear becomes your GPS. And it only has one destination: regret.

Emotional Mastery:

Emotional mastery is the ability to respond—not react—to your emotions.

Picture this: You're driving home after a long day. Someone cuts you off in traffic. Your pulse spikes. You honk, you yell, and you carry that irritation straight into the house. Your spouse says the "wrong" thing. Your kid spills something. A team member sends a frustrating message. You snap—not because of them, but because you were already on edge, and never reset. That's life without emotional mastery.

Now imagine this: same traffic, same day. You notice your tension. You breathe. You let it go. You walk through the door calm, grounded, present. Your family gets your best—not your leftovers. Your team receives clarity instead of chaos.

Emotional mastery doesn't mean suppressing feelings; it means owning your state so others don't have to suffer for it. If you don't master your emotions, they will master you. Left unchecked, emotional reactivity destroys relationships, damages reputations, and ruins opportunities.

Trained daily, it becomes your hidden advantage—fueling leadership, peace, and power. And the truth is, if you don't develop by choice, life will develop it for you—through breakdowns, burnouts, and rock-bottom moments.

Emotional mastery is learned by choice or by crisis. Choose to build it now—before life forces the lesson on you.

Courage:

In your 20s, courage often feels natural. You see the upside, not the risk. You leap because you're driven by what you could gain.

Fast forward 10 or 20 years: a spouse, kids, a mortgage, a team counting on you. The stakes are higher. You start seeing what you could lose—and fear begins to shrink your moves. You play it safe. You wait for more certainty.

But courage isn't reckless; it's calculated risk. It's choosing to move forward even without guarantees—because staying stuck costs more than taking the shot.

Fear whispers *"what if?"*

Courage answers *"even if."*

Without courage, your world contracts. You decline opportunities, avoid growth, and miss breakthroughs. With it, you build momentum, resilience, and a reputation of acting despite fear.

Courage is the muscle that gets you in the room before you feel ready. And the more you train it, the more you realize you were always capable—you just had to go first. Growth doesn't wait for your confidence. It responds to your courage.

The consequence of untrained courage? A life filled with regret, missed chances, and playing below your potential. The reward of training it? Living bold, leading strong, and leaving a legacy that matters.

These three skills—mind mastery, emotional mastery, and courage—are not optional if you want next-level success. They're essential. And like physical strength, they must be trained constantly—not *someday*, not *when things slow down*—but now.

Because if you don't develop them intentionally, life will make you develop them reactively. And that lesson always comes with a higher cost.

You Can't Be a 4 and Expect 10-Level Results

This isn't about worth—it's about capacity. If you want level-10 results in your business, health, or relationships, you must become the level-10 version of you. You don't get to skip growth and still expect greatness. You can't bring a level-4 skill set and expect level-10 results.

It's the entrepreneur trying to scale to $5M with $500K habits—still making every decision, still reacting to fires, still afraid to let go. They don't need a better funnel; they need stronger decision-making, bolder leadership, clearer communication, and deeper self-mastery.

Mastering skills don't guarantee growth—but it creates the capacity for it. It opens the door to scale. But only if you walk through it.

And this is where most people get stuck. They set big goals. They get excited. They take a few actions. And then they stall. Not because they don't care. Not because they aren't trying. But because they haven't yet become the person their goal requires.

That's what cultivating your capacity is all about. And remember: it's not just about how well you execute—it's about how powerfully you lead yourself in every moment.

At the highest levels, everyone knows the strategies. The real difference is self-mastery. That's what separates those who stall… from those who soar.

Who Do You Need to Become?

Here's the question that unlocks everything: *Who do I need to become to live the life I truly want?*

Not just "What do I need to do?"—but *who*. That's the question that reveals the real work.

If your vision is a thriving, low-stress business that gives you freedom and impact, you may need to become a leader who delegates, a person who protects their time, and someone who trusts their team.

If your vision is vibrant health, you may need to become someone who prioritizes rest, plans meals, and trains with consistency.

If your vision is a deeply connected relationship, you may need to become someone who listens more, reacts less, and leads with presence.

Your next level isn't just about better strategy. It's about a better you.

So how do you grow your capacity? First, identify who you need to become. Then identify the skills that version of you requires. Do you need stronger focus? Better emotional regulation? Sharper boundaries?

Here's the key: every skill is a muscle—and like any muscle, it grows through repetition.

If you want to build mind mastery, start noticing your self-talk and challenging disempowering thoughts.

If your goal is to become more proactive, begin each day by identifying your priorities before checking emails or texts.

If you want to lead with more courage, take one small, bold action each day that stretches your comfort zone.

Each repetition builds capacity. Each capacity shift unlocks new results—but in your inner game and in your ability to execute effectively, consistently, and under pressure.

So the next time you say, *"I don't have time,"* stop and ask: *What skill do I need to build to make this easier?*

Time isn't the issue. Skill is.

The good news is that you can develop any skill. You can upgrade any part of yourself. You can grow into your goals— but only if you decide to stop hoping, stop waiting, and stop making excuses. Choose instead to start building you.

You have two choices: keep waiting, keep hoping, keep repeating… or draw the line and declare:

I'm done letting the current version of me dictate the limits of my future. I'm not waiting for permission. I'm not waiting for more time. I'm building me—starting now.

This is where insight becomes transformation—if you're bold enough to act.

Do it now, so your future self looks back with pride—no regrets, no "what ifs."

Reflection Exercise: Step Into Your Next-Level You

Return to the vision you created in Chapter 4, and answer these questions with honesty and precision:

- Who do I need to become to fully live that vision?

- What execution skills, habits, and traits does that version of me embody?

- What self-mastery skills will I need to strengthen to sustain it?

- What's one bold action I can take this week to start becoming that version of me?

Write out your answers. Be specific. This isn't just reflection—it's the blueprint for your next level.

Now that you understand the power of growing your capacity and developing higher-level skills, the next step is ensuring growth isn't just a moment—but a way of life.

Success isn't built on intensity. Success is built on consistency.

In the next chapter, we'll explore the third core element of the Entrepreneur 4C² Success Formula: **Commit to Consistency.**

This is a real game-changer. When you lock in the right routines, rhythms, and momentum, success stops being an event—and starts being automatic.

Turn the page. Let's make **consistency** your superpower.

CHAPTER 6

Why Do You Keep Starting Over?

(Element #3 Commit to Consistency)

*"You will never change your life until
you change something you do daily."*

— John C. Maxwell

What if I told you that everything you've achieved—or failed to achieve—comes down to one thing: your daily routines? Not motivation. Not talent. Not even willpower. Just your routines.

You don't rise to the level of your potential—you fall to the level of your routines. Let that sink in. Because your results will never outgrow your routines.

This is why **Commit to Consistency** is the third core element of the Entrepreneur 4C² Success Formula.

Entrepreneur $4C^2$ Success Formula

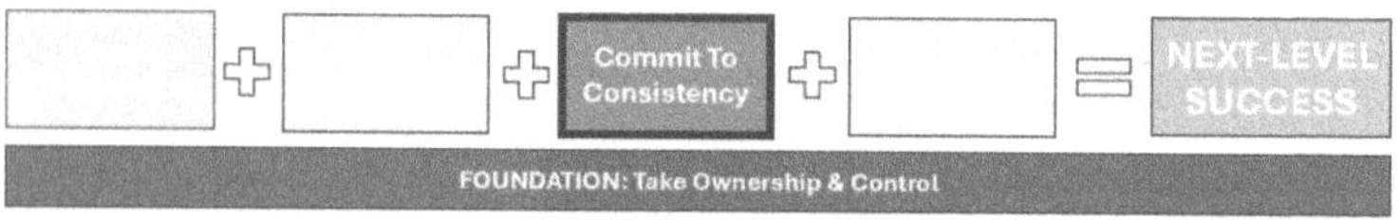

Without consistency, even the best clarity and the strongest capacity fizzle out. Vision fades. Skills go unused. You slip back into old patterns—not because you don't care, but because you lack systems that turn your intentions into action.

Intentions without systems become frustrations.

This is where most entrepreneurs unknowingly lose momentum. But not you—not after this chapter. Because no matter how clear your vision is (*Element #1: Create Congruence*), or how strong your skillset (*Element #2: Cultivate Your Capacity*), none of it sticks without consistent action— automated through powerful systems and habits.

Consistency isn't flashy. But it's the line that divides the stuck from the most successful.

That's what this chapter is all about: Installing the routines that make success your default. Because here's the truth: Whether you realize it or not, you already live by routines.

Did you brush your teeth this morning? Of course you did— though you probably don't remember doing it. You didn't debate, delay, or bargain with yourself. You just did it. That's autopilot.

Now here's what most people never realize: brushing your teeth isn't the exception—it's the rule. **Most of your day already runs on autopilot.**

Think about today. You likely woke up on the same side of the bed, made coffee, brushed your teeth, and checked your phone—just like you always do. You followed the same pattern getting dressed, probably led with the same foot, tied the same shoe first. If you commuted, you stopped at the same gas station or coffee stop, parked in the same spot. You answered emails in your usual rhythm, ate lunch at roughly the same time, and wrapped up your day the way you always do. Then you came home, sat in your familiar chair, and later—without thinking—slid into your usual spot on the couch to watch TV and complete your usual evening routine.

Your entire day—your entire life—is shaped by invisible systems and habits running silently in the background.

And here's the kicker: You don't think about any of it. It just happens—on autopilot.

Your routines are invisible… until they cost you something.

Or you can choose them on purpose—before they choose for you.

And that's the scary part—because autopilot doesn't just apply to brushing your teeth or making coffee. It shapes how you handle stress, lead your team, and make decisions when you're tired, busy, or overwhelmed.

Default behavior creates default outcomes.

This is the *aha* moment for most high-achieving entrepreneurs: your life already runs on systems and routines—you're just not always choosing them consciously.

If you don't choose your routines intentionally, your defaults will choose your future—and those defaults aren't always designed to take you where you want to go.

You've seen it already. Your day is full of routines you didn't choose: morning rituals, work habits, evening wind-downs. Some move you forward. Others quietly hold you back.

And if part of you thinks, *"But I don't want a rigid life full of routines…"* you're not alone. Most entrepreneurs resist structure because they believe it limits their freedom.

But think about it—the routines that already serve you give you freedom every day. You don't wake up debating whether to brush your teeth, shower, or make coffee—you just do it. Those automatic habits remove hundreds of tiny decisions before your day even starts. That's mental freedom.

The truth is simple: **the right systems don't trap you—they free you.**

Structure doesn't kill freedom. It protects it. Systems give you mental bandwidth back. They reduce stress, prevent decision fatigue, and ensure that important actions don't depend on how you feel in the moment.

Want more freedom? More creativity? More time and energy to enjoy your life? Then build better systems and routines.

Because when the right routines run your day, you get to run your life.

The right routines make the results feel effortless.

And here's the best part: you don't need to reinvent your life—you just need to adjust the systems and routines you already have.

Let's be honest. How many times have you:

- Set a bold goal?
- Got excited and started strong?
- And then… faded out and reverted back?

We've all been there.

Maybe it was getting in shape. You bought new workout clothes that made you feel unstoppable. Cleared the pantry. Told yourself and your friends, *"This time it's different."*

And at first—you were on fire. Early workouts. Clean meals. That feeling of momentum building.

Then life happened. A stressful day hit. You skipped a workout. One miss turned into two. Grabbed fast food "just this once." And before long, you were back in old routines—frustrated, disappointed, wondering why it always slips away so fast.

Not because you didn't care. Not because you weren't capable. But because you were relying on self-discipline.

Here's the truth no one tells you (until now): **Self-discipline never works—at least not for long**. It's one of the biggest myths in entrepreneurship.

Think about it. What's the definition of self-discipline? Forcing yourself to do something you don't want to do.

Who's going to do that—every day, indefinitely? No one. Not you. Not me. Not anyone.

You can't build a lifestyle on force. You build it on flow. But most people don't. They make success harder than it needs to be—relying on pressure instead of process.

It's a myth that's been sold for years: *hustle harder, push through, and grind no matter what.* But that approach burns out even the best of us.

Self-discipline is like a phone battery. You wake up charged, ready to go. Then stress, surprises, and setbacks drain it fast. By afternoon, you're running on 5%—defaulting to old habits.

That's why the real secret isn't more discipline. It's better systems and routines.

Systems don't care how you feel—they just execute.

This isn't about being lazy or unmotivated. It's about being strategic.

Results follow your systems, not your intentions.

And when those systems are rock solid, they carry you forward even on your worst day. Success isn't about perfection—it's about what your systems do when everything goes sideways.

Which raises a simple question: **what's the difference between a routine and a system?**

Here's the distinction:

- **Routines** are the actions you want to repeat.
- **Systems** are what make sure you repeat them.

Think of routines as the "what" and systems as the "how." Together, they automate your success.

For example: A routine would be deciding to make 10 outbound sales calls each weekday.

The system is what makes that routine inevitable—a protected 9:00–11:00 a.m. prospecting block on your calendar, your lead list prepped the night before, your script and CRM open at 9:00 sharp, a simple target ("10 dials / 2 real conversations"), and a quick 11:05 check-in to send your numbers to an accountability partner.

That's why discipline alone will never be enough.

Discipline is admirable—but unreliable.

You need a backup plan for the days life throws punches.

Systems and routines are that plan.

They're the safety net that turns chaos into control—and ambition into action.

Now it's time to optimize your plan—so your systems and routines create the success and freedom you desire.

Step 1: Upgrade What Already Exists

Here's the good news: you don't need to overhaul your life. This isn't about changing everything—it's about changing one thing at a time and letting that one win compound.

You simply need to look at what you're already doing—and make small, strategic upgrades.

Because the biggest wins are built on the smallest tweaks.

Say every afternoon around 3 p.m., you hit a slump and grab something sugary to stay alert. What if you swapped that sugar hit for a three-minute walk and a tall glass of water? Same routine—just upgraded.

Or maybe you spend evenings passively watching whatever's on TV.

What if you turned one of those nights into a "goal night" where you review your vision and prep for the week ahead?

These aren't massive changes. They're tiny shifts to routines you already have. But over time, they create extraordinary results.

Here's where most entrepreneurs go wrong: they try to upgrade *everything* at once. They go from zero workouts to five-a-week, from no structure to a 90-minute morning routine overnight. It's unsustainable.

The secret isn't speed—it's installation.

Start microscopic.

Five pushups a day for a month.

One gratitude text.

A single three-minute walk.

You're not building the habit's *outcome* yet—you're building the *autopilot*. Once that's locked in, *then* you stack and grow.

Step 2: Anchor New Habits to Existing Ones

Once you've optimized what's already in place, then—and only then—should you add new routines. The easiest way to build them is to **anchor them to something you already do on autopilot.**

For example:

- If you want to boost your creativity, as soon as you sit in your desk chair each morning, jot down one new idea as a single line in your idea list.

- To deepen your relationships, as soon as you touch your phone each morning, send a one-sentence text to one contact naming one thing you respect about them— before anything else.

- If you want to stretch more, do 30 seconds of stretching while waiting for the shower to heat up.

These are tiny—almost laughably simple. But the secret is repetition until they become automatic. And the easiest way to make that happen is to attach them to something you already do without thinking.

If it's simple enough to skip, it's powerful enough to change you—*if* done consistently.

Neuroscience proves it: the brain loves patterns. Repeat a behavior often enough, and it shifts from effort to autopilot—conserving energy while improving performance.

That's why tiny upgrades don't just feel easier… they are easier, over time. When anchored to existing habits, they require almost no effort to remember.

The goal is never the action itself.

The goal is to hardwire it into your routine.

Take one entrepreneur we worked with who wanted sharper focus in the afternoons. Instead of relying on willpower, he built a "reset ritual" every day at 2pm—anchored to the buzz of his smartwatch alarm.

When it went off, he'd stand up, take three deep breaths, and ask himself one question:

"What matters most in the next hour?"

That small ritual transformed his afternoons. Instead of spiraling into distractions, he re-centered and made powerful progress. Within two months, he doubled his afternoon productivity and finally finished a project he'd been delaying for nearly a year.

No discipline. Just a system.

A 30-second habit changed a year-long outcome.

Your Routines = Your Results

Here's the truth:

Eat healthy consistently → You get healthy results. Move your body consistently → You feel strong and energized. Focus on business priorities consistently → Your business grows. Invest in your relationships consistently → They flourish.

And the reverse is just as true:

Hit snooze, scroll first thing in the morning, delay important tasks, react instead of lead—and your results will reflect that too.

You don't get what you *want*—you get what you *repeat*.

Your routines form the foundation of your results—good or bad. And the right systems ensure those routines happen, especially on days you don't feel like it.

That's the defining difference between struggling entrepreneurs and thriving ones:

Thriving entrepreneurs choose their routines with intention—and build the systems to support them.

You Before the Queue

One of the most powerful systems we teach entrepreneurs is **You Before the Queue**—a morning block that puts you first and makes everything after it easier.

The "queue" is the world waiting in line for your attention: your phone, inbox, notifications, staff, and clients—all asking for a piece of you. **You Before the Queue** is how you take your power back.

Think of it as a quiet pocket of intention before the world can ask you for a single thing. **No phone. No email. No social media. No staff. No clients.**

Before the world gets access to you—you take care of YOU.

- You feed your mind.
- You fuel your body.
- You nurture your relationships.
- You take bold action on your business.

Then—and only then—let the queue in.

You don't need more hours in the day—you need better hours at the start of it.

Here's what that might look like:

- **Mind:** Read a few pages of an inspiring book or spend five minutes visualizing your next win.

- **Body:** Walk around the block, do a set of jumping jacks, or small workout with weights.

- **Relationships:** Leave a sticky note with a kind message for someone at home or send a voice message to a friend.

- **Business:** Spend 30+ minutes making progress on a high-priority project—before checking any messages.

During this time, you are unavailable to the world. No phone. No social media. No inbox.

When you put you first, the world gets the best of you—not what's left over.

You train the world to wait because you've chosen to prioritize yourself.

Take one entrepreneur we worked with. She would wake up stressed, dive into emails, and feel like she was chasing her day from the get-go. Her mornings felt like a sprint she never signed up for.

Then she adopted a simple "You Before the Queue" routine: five minutes of reading from a mindset book, 15 squats, one note of appreciation to her partner, and 60 minutes on her top business priority—before checking her phone or email.

The shift was immediate. Her mornings went from reactive to powerful. Within weeks, her energy, focus, and business results skyrocketed. She didn't change her business—she changed her morning routine. Same life. Different start. That's the power of choosing your routine.

Even many celebrities and elite performers follow this pattern. Take Dwayne "The Rock" Johnson: despite running businesses, filming movies, and raising a family, he starts every day with his own *You Before the Queue* routine—training, eating clean, and getting focused before giving the world his attention.

That's not luck. That's a system.

Success doesn't happen to him. It happens because of him.

And it's why he continues to perform at an elite level year after year.

The exact timing doesn't matter—maybe it's 8 a.m., maybe it's 11. What matters is **consistency**. Because in the end, your routines don't just shape your day—**they shape your destiny.**

The Compounding Power of Tiny Upgrades

If you made just two small routine upgrades each month—improving an existing habit or adding a new one—you'd create 24 positive shifts in a year.

Now imagine the impact of 24 automatic, aligned actions on your health, business, relationships, energy, and mindset.

That's the power of systems and routines. Each change may feel small in the moment, but compounded over time, it creates extraordinary transformation—without willpower, stress, or constantly starting over.

Think of these upgrades like compound interest. At first, growth is invisible. Then suddenly—it's exponential. Each small win stacks on the last, until your routines are earning interest on your success.

Momentum doesn't come from motivation—it comes from mastering routines. That's how high performers build unstoppable progress: not overnight, but every single day.

You have a choice: continue relying on motivation and waiting for the perfect time, doing what you've always done—or choose to build the system now, so your next win is inevitable, not accidental.

Your Next Step: Design Your First Upgrade

Don't wait for motivation. Design your upgrade right now. This is where you shift from knowing to doing.

Reflect for a moment:

- What's one routine you already do daily that you could improve with a tiny adjustment?

- What's one new habit you want—and what can you anchor it to?

- What would your *You Before the Queue* routine look like? Include something for your mind, body, relationships, and business.

Start small. Make it automatic. Repeat it every day for the next 30 days—and watch what happens.

Because when your routines change—everything changes.

Picture this: 30 days from now, you wake up calm, focused, and energized—because your day starts with intention. You've stopped chasing motivation and started living results that last—not because life got easier, but because your system got smarter.

Smart systems beat strong willpower every time. That's the power of choosing systems that support your success—even when life doesn't.

You've now seen how to create small, powerful routines that run on autopilot—and how those changes multiply over time. But even the strongest routines can only carry you so far alone.

If you want to scale your results, expand your impact, and grow further and faster than you ever could solo— you need the final core element of the Entrepreneur 4C^2 Success Formula: **Champion Collaboration**

In the next chapter, we'll explore how the most successful entrepreneurs build aligned relationships and leverage synergy to create results no one could achieve alone.

Consistency builds momentum—collaboration makes it exponential.

CHAPTER 7

What If You're Not Meant to Do This Alone?

(Element #4 Champion Collaboration)

*"You can have it all. You just
can't do it all by yourself."*

— SARA BLAKELY

What if the fastest way to accelerate your success wasn't grinding harder… but multiplying your momentum with the right people?

You've already done the work. You've created congruence, cultivated your capacity, and committed to consistency. You've sparked the flame. Now it's time to accelerate it—not by pushing harder, but by pulling others in.

Because this next level? You don't get there alone. Solo strength got you here. Shared strength gets you where you want to go.

That's why the fourth and final element of the Entrepreneur 4C² Success Formula isn't optional—it's essential: **Champion Collaboration.**

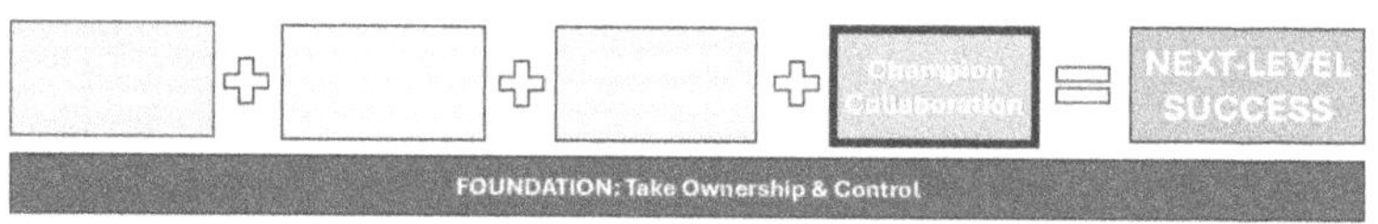

No matter how skilled, motivated, or aligned you are... you will never reach next-level success alone. Sure, you can achieve some wins on your own. But extraordinary results? Explosive growth? That requires others.

Independence builds resilience—but collaboration builds empires.

Collaboration isn't a side strategy—it's the accelerator.

Too many entrepreneurs waste years guarding turf instead of building alliances. The most successful do the opposite. They reframe every "competitor" as a collaborator-in-waiting. While most play a zero-sum game—*Who can I beat? Who's getting more attention? How do I take more of the market?*—the top performers flip the question:

"How can we grow together?"

Competition creates limits; collaboration removes them. And it's not just a strategy—it's a mindset, a default way of operating.

When you adopt this mindset, opportunities appear everywhere:

- **In business**—through partnerships, co-creations, and shared audiences

- **In your internal team**—by aligning, focusing, and building together

- **In your home**—through deeper communication with your spouse or family

- **In your circle**—by connecting with expanders who help you grow

The most successful entrepreneurs make collaboration a core part of their strategy—because the right relationship can achieve what no strategy alone ever could.

You've done the hard work. You've built the fire—vision, skills, and systems. But fire alone burns out. Collaboration is the fuel. You don't need to burn brighter; you need to burn together.

One aligned partnership, conversation, or connection can ignite momentum that would've taken years to build solo. A single relationship can double your reach, multiply revenue, or finally break through the ceiling you've been hitting.

That's why Champion Collaboration isn't a bonus—it's your multiplier. One aligned partnership can collapse five years of struggle into one year of growth.

And here's the truth: this isn't about asking for help. It's about unlocking exponential results through strategic alignment. The most successful entrepreneurs don't collaborate occasionally—they collaborate intentionally, consistently, and without ego.

McDonald's Didn't Grow Alone—And Neither Will You

Most think McDonald's scaled because of systems. Not exactly. Systems scaled the operations—but collaboration built the empire. McDonald's succeeded because of partnerships.

McDonald's didn't try to "do it all themselves." They built a franchise model, enabling thousands of entrepreneurs to collaborate under one brand. They partnered with real estate experts to secure prime locations and coordinated with local vendors, franchisees, and strategic suppliers to scale globally.

Without those collaborations, McDonald's wouldn't be McDonald's.

That's the power of collaboration—not just adding partners, but multiplying results. And it doesn't only happen at global scale

Take a neighborhood yoga studio. They partnered with the café next door to launch a 30-day **Move + Brew Challenge**:

- The studio sold a punch card that included weekly coffee vouchers.
- The café hosted Saturday community classes.
- Both promoted through their lists and socials.

The outcome? The studio filled its off-peak classes and sold more memberships. The café gained new regulars. Two small businesses turned two small audiences into one thriving community—without changing their core offers.

That's collaboration. Simple. Smart. Scalable.

Your Circle Is Your Shortcut

You've probably heard the old saying: *"You are the average of the five people you spend the most time with."* It's true. Your environment shapes your energy, your beliefs, and your standards.

When you surround yourself with collaborators who challenge and stretch you, your capacity expands faster. Growth accelerates when your circle raises your ceiling. But stay around people who play small, complain, or stay stuck—and your success will stall too.

The fastest way to upgrade your business and life? **Upgrade your circle**.

You don't just outgrow people—you outgrow patterns. And often, the people are tied to those patterns. That doesn't mean abandoning current relationships. It means intentionally seeking new ones that reflect where you want to rise to.

- Want to be more focused? Spend time with people who value time and protect their priorities.

- Want to grow your business faster? Connect with those who've already done it— and are happy to help you shorten the path.

Proximity creates possibility. The right people don't just inspire you—they normalize excellence. They hold you to a higher standard simply by living it.

Collaboration starts with proximity. You don't need all the answers—just access to better questions. You don't need more hustle—you need more access.

You're Not Supposed to Do This Alone

Entrepreneurs often wear the badge of "I'll do it myself" with pride, believing success comes from solo grit and endless grind. But doing it alone doesn't make you strong—it makes you slow.

Isolation looks noble—until it costs you everything.

We've been taught that real success is forged in solitude. It isn't. Isolation doesn't build legacies—it builds burnout. It builds regrets: the help you didn't invite, the time you didn't save, the wins you didn't share.

When you collaborate, you:

- Leverage strengths you don't have

- Share the load—and the wins

- Expand your reach, impact, and opportunities

- Build momentum faster than you ever could alone

You don't lose control through collaboration—you gain opportunity.

Want to see it in action? A leadership coach partners with a podcast host to create a limited audio series—reaching thousands of new listeners on both sides. A product-based business teams up with a graphic designer to rebrand their packaging—doubling engagement and visibility. Two local business owners cross-promote each other's services through a referral incentive—one gains new leads, the other builds stronger retention.

These collaborations work because they're not about "me"— they're about "we." Trade ego for alignment, and everyone wins.

The Real Estate Flip That Changed Everything

John had been investing in real estate for years. He did it all himself—finding properties, managing rehabs, dealing with subs, negotiating with lenders. He was profitable, but exhausted. Every project dragged on. Every flip felt like a grind.

Then he met Bill—a general contractor with crews and years of hands-on experience. Bill wasn't an investor, but he was fast, reliable, and delivered quality work ahead of schedule.

They teamed up on one flip: John handled the deal and financing; Bill ran the renovation start to finish. The house sold in record time—with higher-than-expected profits.

One project turned into five. Then ten. Their business exploded. John stopped juggling subs and started scaling. Bill stopped chasing one-off jobs and became a partner in a thriving company. It was a win-win. They stayed in their lanes—and went further, faster, together.

Sometimes your breakthrough isn't more effort—it's the right ally.

The lesson? John didn't need to do more. He needed someone great at what he wasn't. That's what collaboration unlocks— exponential growth through shared strengths.

Collaboration Applies to Every Area of Life.

This isn't just about business. Collaboration fuels growth everywhere.

When you collaborate with your spouse, you co-create a shared vision, support each other's goals, and lead as a team. When you collaborate with your team, ask what they need to win— then build it together. When you collaborate with friends and mentors, share your vision. Don't hide it. The right people will want to help.

And when you collaborate with other entrepreneurs—don't try to do everything. Find those with complementary strengths and build together.

You don't need to carry it all—you just need to stop carrying it alone.

This Isn't Optional—It's non-negotiable.

Champion Collaboration isn't something you try once. It's not a box to check or a bonus strategy. It's a way of operating—a mindset that turns connection into acceleration.

Just like the first three elements of the 4C² Success Formula, this one must be practiced.

Regularly ask yourself:

- Who am I building with?

- Are we aligned?

- Where can we combine forces?

- Who else should be in my circle?

If you want to go far, collaboration can't be an event—it must become a way of life.

Make Collaboration a Practice

Don't wait until you're stuck. Build with others before you hit the wall. Make it a habit. A pattern. An instinct.

Don't wait for collapse to create connection—build it now. When you do, everything gets lighter. Success moves faster. Fulfilment deepens. Because now, you're building with *fuel*, not *friction*.

Business isn't built in isolation. Neither is life. The sooner you embrace collaboration, the faster everything accelerates.

Reflection Exercise: Start Collaborating Like a Pro

Take a few minutes to reflect honestly on the following:

- Who in your business, network, or personal life is aligned with your vision—but underutilized?

- What collaboration could accelerate your goals—if you simply started the conversation?

- Where are you still trying to do everything yourself—and what's it costing you?

- Who expands your thinking, sharpens your focus, or fuels your energy– and how can you spend more time with them?

- Which area of your life—business, health, or relationships—would benefit most from collaboration, and who could you invite in?

Now take action.

Reach out to one person today—someone who complements your strengths, believes in your vision, or can help you accelerate.

Collaboration isn't luck—it's a choice. Make that choice now, so your future self isn't left with the regret of, *"I should have asked for help."*

At this point, you've built your foundation **(Take Ownership & Control)** and activated all four core elements of the Entrepreneur 4C² Success Formula:

1. **Create Congruence**

2. **Cultivate Capacity**

3. **Commit to Consistency**

4. **Champion Collaboration**

But there's one final step you must lock in. Embed these elements into your daily life—until they become *who you are.*

In the next chapter, you'll learn the **SUCCESS Operating System**—a seven-step framework that anchors your foundation and integrates all four core elements of the **4C² Succcess Formula,** so they run on autopilot in every area of life.

Real transformation doesn't come from trying harder—it comes from installing a system that makes next-level success your default.

You've done the work.

Now let's make it permanent.

CHAPTER 8

Can You Make Your Success Inevitable?

(The 7-Step SUCCESS Operating System)

"Systems run the business.
People run the systems."

— MICHAEL GERBER

What if success didn't depend on motivation, willpower, or luck—but was *inevitable*? Predictable. Repeatable. Scalable?

You weren't meant to chase success—you were meant to live it. And the way you live it is by installing a system that makes success automatic.

Up to this point, you've built your foundation and mastered the four core elements of the Entrepreneur $4C^2$ Success Formula.

Entrepreneur $4C^2$ Success Formula

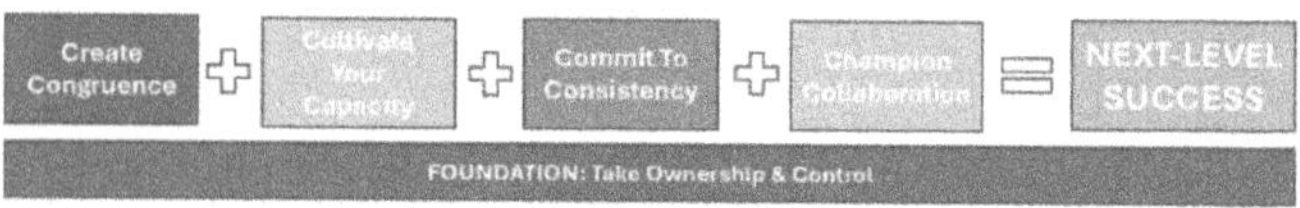

You've seen how the foundation and each element work together—each unlocking a unique dimension of your next-level success. Like the reels on a jackpot machine, when all five align, you hit the ultimate payout: the life and business you've been building toward.

But if even one is missing, your results falter. You might still find some success, but not the kind that feels sustainable, scalable, or deeply fulfilling. The more gaps there are, the more you'll experience struggle, setbacks, and eventual burnout.

The real win only happens when all five are aligned—working together as one unified system.

So the real challenge is: how do you keep all five active and aligned—every single day?

The top 10% of entrepreneurs don't rely on hope; they run an *operating system* that makes success automatic. Knowing the formula creates **potential**. Installing it creates **predictable success**. It's not what you know that changes your life—it's what you *execute*.

So how do you execute it—consistently, automatically, every single day?

That's where the **7-Step SUCCESS Operating System** comes in. It's the repeatable system that keeps your foundation and all four core elements active and aligned—so success stops being random and becomes predictable, on schedule.

We've seen hundreds of entrepreneurs use this system to sharpen their focus, multiply growth, and reclaim control of their business and life. Now, it's your turn.

Think of the $4C^2$ Success Formula as the engine that drives next-level results—and the SUCCESS Operating System as the *ignition key* that starts it every time. You'll install it live in seven moves—**S-U-C-C-E-S-S**—so alignment, execution, and adjustment run daily on repeat.

This framework draws directly from how the most successful leaders operate—turning extraordinary results into a consistent outcome, not an occasional event.

Now it's time to install it. The engine's built—turn the key.

The 7-Step SUCCESS Operating System

This operating system ensures your foundation and all four core elements of the $4C^2$ Success Formula *stay installed, active, and aligned*—consistently, across every area of life and business where you want extraordinary results.

Each step integrates the $4C^2$ Success Formula into your daily life in a way that's simple, repeatable, and proven to work. Together, these seven steps form the acronym **S.U.C.C.E.S.S.**—a clear, memorable framework that keeps you focused on what matters most and executing with precision.

It's both your compass and your autopilot: keeping you on course and in motion, every day, in every area that matters most. Whether in business, health, or relationships, this system aligns every moving part so results happen—without guesswork, burnout, or wasted effort.

One entrepreneur told me privately that he was burned out after years of long hours and constant pressure. Within weeks of following the system, his schedule stabilized, his income held steady, and he began rebuilding his health and marriage.

That's the power of this system. Follow the steps, and watch your results compound.

Here's how it works:

Each of the seven steps in this operating system is a gear in the machine. Miss one, and the momentum stalls. Engage them all, and success becomes inevitable.

The beauty of the SUCCESS Operating System lies in its flexibility. It's not tied to a single goal or area—it works wherever you want extraordinary results: business, health, relationships, friendships—any area of your life.

And because it's flexible, the fastest way to *understand* it is to install it—not analyze it—in one area right now.

Why Do It Now

Reading doesn't change your life—*running the system* does.

If you keep turning pages without acting, you train your brain to confuse learning with progress. Not here. Not today.

This is where most people stop at "good ideas." They nod, highlight, and drift back to the same habits, the same chaos, the same results. Don't be that person. The cost of inaction isn't just frustration—it's the opportunity your family, your team, and your future lose when you hold back your full potential.

Every hour you delay installing this system is an hour of clarity, momentum, and freedom you could already have. You don't need more information—you need *implementation*.

One decision. One hour. Real momentum. Real change.

Before We Dive In

Pick one area of your business or life to focus on. You'll apply each step of the SUCCESS Operating System to that single area as you read.

Need help installing this as you go? The free AI Success Strategist is here to help you implement now—not just highlight and move on. Use it for quick prompts, troubleshooting, or to turn your notes into actions in minutes.

Go to: https://www.NextLevelSuccessInstitute.com/ai

Or scan the QR code below:

The Live Challenge: Don't read this—run it now

1. Set aside 45–60 focused minutes.

2. Silence distractions—phone off, notifications off, door closed.

3. Grab a pen and one sheet of paper (or open a blank document).

4. Decide: *"I'm not just learning the system. I'm installing it—right now."*

5. Choose a small reward for completing it—and a real consequence if you don't.

Follow each step in real time as you read. By the end of this chapter, you won't just *understand* the SUCCESS Operating System—you'll have *run it once, live,* and created tangible momentum.

Don't let this be another book that inspires you but doesn't change you.

Do it once—right now—and you'll never look at success the same way again.

Got your focus area? Good. Let's begin.

1. S—Seize Ownership & Control

The first step in this operating system is **ownership**. Examine the area you choose now. Every result you have—and every result you don't—exists because of you. Not the economy. Not your team. Not your spouse. Not your circumstances. **You**.

Ownership means refusing to blame others or hide behind circumstances. It's choosing to face the mirror.

Do it now (3 minutes): List three results in this area you've been blaming on external factors.

Decide (2 minutes): Rewrite each as "I own ___. I will ___ next."

Your results reflect your actions—or inaction. From today forward, ask yourself:

"How can I change this? What will I do differently now?"

But ownership alone isn't enough. You must also take **control**. That means declaring:

From this moment forward, I'm in charge of what happens here. No excuses. No waiting. No blame. I decide. I act. I create.

I've seen this pattern countless times with real estate investors. Many master one strategy—say, flipping—and thrive while the market's hot. However, as soon as the market conditions change, they crash and blame "the market." But the truth is that the markets always change. It's not *if*—it's *when*. And this isn't unique to real estate—every industry shifts: ad costs spike, algorithms change, supply chains slip.

Every time they do, you see investors complaining, struggling, going out of business. But there are also those who take control. They own the result. They study the shift, face the facts, and rewrite the plan. They don't tweak the strategy—they reinvent it to match reality. They don't wait for the market to be kind; they redesign their approach and reinvent themselves.

They choose their future instead of letting the market choose it for them.

That's control.

Here's what shifts when you do:

- You move from **reactive** (waiting, blaming, excusing) to **proactive** (choosing, creating, directing).

- You stop treating goals as "hopes" and start making them musts.

- You draw a line in the sand and declare: *This is my responsibility. I will get the results. Nothing will stop me.*

Commitment Check

Write your answers. Make it real.

1. **What situation am I taking full ownership of from this point forward?** *(e.g., "the performance of this team," "the state of my marriage," "my current health trajectory.")*

2. **What is 100% within my control here?** *(List three levers: decisions, standards, conversations, boundaries, plans.)*

3. **What decision am I making today to take control?** *(Name the decision and the first move you will make in the next 24 hours.)*

4. **What blame story am I retiring right now—and what's my ownership statement instead?** *(Write one sentence: "I'm done blaming ____. From now on: I choose __/will __.")*

5. **Control protocol:** *When* **[trigger]** *happens, I will* **[specific action]** *within 15 minutes. (Example: "When I catch myself blaming the market, I'll pause, ask 'What can I control?' pick one lever, and act.")*

This is the foundation. Without it, nothing else sticks. With it, you gain the power to create results on demand—because you've reclaimed the one thing that matters most: **control over yourself.**

Do not move on until you've truly taken ownership. Not halfway. Not in theory.

Write it. Feel it. Decide it.

Because every step that follows will only work if *you* are in the driver's seat. If you skip this, the system becomes information. When you own it, it becomes transformation.

Take a deep breath. Reread your ownership statements. Lock them in.

This is the moment you take back your power.

Now that you've seized ownership and control… it's time to unlock your **Inner Compass**.

2. U—Unlock Your Inner Compass

Control without direction leads to exhaustion. You can drive faster than ever—and still end up at the wrong destination.

That's not a speed problem; it's an aim problem.

Most people chase the wrong goals—set by ego, pressure, or comparison—and grind toward outcomes that don't fulfill them. That's why, after seizing ownership and control, the next step is to pause, strip away the noise, and get crystal clear on what you really want in the one area you're focusing on right now.

Look closely at this area of your life—whether it's your business, health, relationships, or finances and—ask yourself the question that cuts through ego, fear, and expectation:

"If I only had six months left and had to look back at this area with no do-overs… what would I regret not doing, not experiencing, or not becoming?"

This is not about what looks good on paper or what others expect of you. It's about the truth. Your truth.

Do it now (7 minutes):

1. Answer the six-month question in **3–5 raw sentences** (present tense, no polishing).

2. **Name 1–3 core feelings** you want most in this area (e.g., strong, free, connected).

3. **Write a 3–5 sentence vision** of this area as you want it to look and feel.

4. **Spot the ego:** circle anything about proving or impressing; **rewrite it** so it serves your truth.

Now sharpen your vision with these examples—use them to refine, not replace, what you wrote.

If your focus area is **health**, looking back you probably wouldn't regret missing a certain "goal weight" or forcing yourself into yet another restrictive diet. What you'd truly regret might sound more like:

- *"I wish I had the energy to play with my kids without feeling exhausted."*
- *"I wish I had felt confident in my own skin instead of hiding."*
- *"I wish I had taken care of my body so I could live longer and love better."*

If your focus area is **business**, you wouldn't regret not adding another zero to your revenue. But you might regret:

- *"I wish I had built a business that gave me freedom instead of chaining me to my desk."*
- *"I wish I had led with purpose, not just pressure."*

If it's **relationships**, you wouldn't regret not having more followers on social media. You might regret:

- *"I wish I had listened more deeply to the people I love."*
- *"I wish I had created more memories instead of more excuses."*

If it's **finances**, you wouldn't regret not buying another luxury car. You might regret:

- *"I wish I had created security and peace instead of living under constant stress."*
- *"I wish I had used money as a tool for freedom, not just as a scorecard."*

That's the difference between **ego goals** and **true vision**. Ego goals are about proving something. Real vision is about *living* something.

Keep your feelings and vision paragraph handy—you'll use them in Steps 3–7.

This becomes your Inner Compass— the North Star that will guide every step that follows. When your actions align with it, motivation becomes effortless. You're no longer chasing success—you're being pulled toward a life that actually matters to you.

Pause here. Re-read what you wrote. Feel the truth in it. Because from this point forward, everything you build must align with this compass—or you'll drift right back into misaligned effort.

You've taken ownership. You've found direction. Now it's time to build the strength, focus, and self-mastery to stay on course—no matter what challenges appear next.

3. C—Cultivate Next-Level Self-Mastery & Execution Skills

Now comes the hardest—and most rewarding—part: becoming the person capable of living it.

Clarity without growth changes nothing. The next question now is: **Are you the version of yourself capable of fully living this vision out?**

This is where growth becomes non-negotiable. Because here's the truth: your results will never rise higher than your capacity. Your health won't transform beyond your ability to sustain it. Your relationships won't deepen beyond your ability to connect. Your freedom won't expand beyond your ability to manage it. And your business won't grow beyond your ability to lead it.

This is the moment to look in the mirror and ask the most important question of all:

"Who do I need to become to live this vision fully?"

This isn't about superficial upgrades—it's about identity. The next level of results demands the next level of *you*.

Capacity isn't one-dimensional. To reach your next level, you must honestly identify and develop two sets of skills: self-mastery skills and execution skills. Self-mastery skills may include mindset, emotional regulation, courage, focus, and resilience. Execution skills on the other hand involves communication, leadership, influence, planning, and follow-through.

You need both. If you only develop one side, you will never build the capacity required to fully achieve your vision. Self-mastery skills give you the resilience and presence to stay grounded under pressure, while execution skills give you the ability to act, implement, and follow through.

Only by cultivating both will you unlock your true capacity.

Do it now (8 minutes):

1. **Identity check**: *Who do I need to become to live this vision fully?* Write it in one bold, declarative paragraph.

2. **Identify your gap**: List the self-mastery and execution skills you currently have in this area, then list the ones missing or underdeveloped.

3. **Pick your power skills**: Circle the top one inner skill and one outer skill that—if improved—would make the biggest difference toward your vision.

Here's the shift: you don't *achieve* goals—you *grow into* them.

For example:

- If your vision is vibrant health, your missing skills might be **energy mastery** (inner) and **meal planning** (outer).

- If it's a thriving business, your gaps might be **courage** (inner) and **delegation** (outer).

- If you want deeper relationships, you might need **emotional mastery** (inner) and **listening** (outer).

Capacity is like a muscle—it grows through intentional training, not wishful thinking. Every rep you put in—whether mastering your thoughts, strengthening your resilience, improving communication, or sharpening leadership—builds the version of you required for your next level.

Your next breakthrough in this area of life won't come from a new tactic or a lucky break. It will come from upgrading the person who's showing up to run the play.

Pause for a moment and look at what you just wrote. That identity paragraph? That's the blueprint for your next evolution.

You've taken ownership. You've found clarity. Now you're becoming the person capable of living it.

The next step is to give that version of you a clear, strategic plan to win—because growth without direction becomes chaos, and power without a plan leads to wasted potential.

4. C—Create & Implement Effective Strategies & Goals

Now it's time to decide *how* you'll get there. This is where clarity becomes practical. A vision without strategy is just a wish—and skills without practice never become real.

Your job now is simple: choose the few strategies and goals that will move you closer to your vision *while* building the skills you need to sustain it. Both matter.

Think of it this way. Your vision points to where you're going. Your skills determine who you must become to get there. Your strategies and goals form the bridge between who you are and who you're becoming.

For example:

- If your vision is vibrant health, your strategies might be to lift weights three times a week, avoid sugar six days a week, and get at least seven hours of sleep each night.

- If your vision is a deeply connected marriage, your strategies might be to plan a weekly date night, spend ten distraction-free minutes connecting each day, and speak one word of appreciation daily.

- If your vision is financial freedom, your strategies might be to save a set percentage of income, eliminate high-interest debt, and review spending weekly.

And just as important, your strategies should directly develop the skills you identified in Step 3. For example:

- To build courage, take one bold action each week that stretches you.

- To strengthen emotional mastery, pause before responding in high-pressure situations.

- To grow focus, block protected time for your highest-priority work.

- To develop resilience, reframe every setback into a lesson the same day it occurs.

Notice how these strategies are clear, simple, and measurable. They don't describe *how* you'll do it—they define *what* you will do.

Do it now (10 minutes):

1. **Choose:** Identify 3–5 specific strategies that would move you toward your vision *and* 3-5 more to build your chosen inner and outer skills.

2. **Refine:** For each strategy, write a clear, measurable goal (e.g., "Plan one date night every Friday," not "Spend more time together").

3. **Commit:** Circle the top 1–3 strategies that will make the biggest difference, and commit to focusing on them first.

This step isn't about doing everything. It's about identifying the vital few strategies and goals that matter most—and making them real.

Write them down. This is your playbook. These strategies and goals will form the foundation of the systems and routines we'll create in Step 5.

Because here's the truth: your vision won't be achieved through hope or willpower. It will be achieved through a handful of clear strategies—executed with consistency—until they become your default way of operating.

You've chosen your direction and designed your plan. Now it's time to make it automatic.

5. E—Establish Empowering Systems & Routines

You already know this truth from earlier: you don't rise to the level of your potential—you fall to the level of your routines. Success doesn't depend on motivation or willpower. It's built on systems and routines that make the right actions automatic.

This step is where your vision, skills, and strategies stop being ideas and start becoming reality. Without routines, even the best strategies fade. With them, success becomes your default—especially on your worst days.

Do it now (10–12 minutes):

1. **Map:** For each of your top 1–3 strategies from Step 4, write **one routine** that would make it automatic.

2. **Design:** Give each routine a **time, place, and trigger**—anchor it to something you already do.

3. **Install:** Add each routine to your **calendar (set to recur)**, attach **one reminder or trigger**, and **automate** where possible.

Examples—turning strategies into systems:

- If your strategy is to work out three times a week, your routine could be locking those sessions into your calendar every Monday, Wednesday, and Friday at the same time.

- If your strategy is to strengthen your relationship with your spouse, your routine could be anchoring a nightly 10-minute connection to the moment you plug your phone in to charge.

- If your strategy is to save a set percentage of income, your system could be automating the transfer before you ever see the money.

Now apply the same approach to your skill-building strategies:

- If your strategy is to build courage, your routine could be scheduling a weekly "fear rep" where you deliberately do one bold thing that stretches you.

- If your strategy is to strengthen emotional mastery, your routine could be a daily reset ritual—anchored to a trigger like closing your laptop or hearing a calendar alarm.

- If your strategy is to grow focus, your routine could be protecting a sacred 90-minute deep-work block at the same time every day.

- If your strategy is to develop resilience, your routine could be journaling one lesson from every setback before bed.

The Key: Installation (Do this now)

1. Put the routines in your calendar (recurring).

2. **Add one trigger** for each (anchor or reminder).

3. **Set one automation** if relevant (e.g., transfers, scheduled messages).

Because here's the truth: **self-discipline fades. Systems don't.** Once you establish empowering routines—and actually install them—you stop *hoping* for change and start *living* it.

Pause here. You've built your foundation, your vision, your identity, your strategies, and your systems. Now imagine what happens when you connect all of that power to other people who share your drive.

That's where the real acceleration begins.

6. S—Synergize to Thrive

Up to this point, the work has been personal. But your vision will always hit a ceiling if you try to carry it alone.

The next level isn't about working harder—it's about working together.

Synergy is what multiplies everything you've built so far. One aligned partner, ally, or supporter can compress years of trial and error into months of progress. The right person doesn't just lighten your load—they expand what's possible.

You've created momentum; now it's time to connect that momentum to others who amplify it.

This step is about proactively bringing others in to help you accelerate growth, expand capacity, and realize your vision faster than you ever could on your own.

Do it now (8–10 minutes):

1. **Identify:** List 3–5 people, partners, or communities who could support, accelerate, or complement your vision in this area. *(Think mentors, peers, team members, friends, coaches, strategic collaborators.)*

   Prompts: Who could I invite to support or accelerate this vision? Who already has the strengths I lack—or the wisdom I need? Where am I trying to do everything myself, and what is it costing me?

2. **Assess:** For each, note the strengths, resources, or perspectives they bring that you don't currently have.

3. **Act:** Choose 1–2 and take immediate action—send a message, schedule a conversation, or make a specific ask.

Examples in action:

- **Health:** Partner with a trainer or accountability buddy who keeps you consistent.

- **Relationships:** Co-create a shared ritual with your spouse (e.g., a weekly date night or daily connection practice).

- **Finances:** Work with a coach, advisor, or accountability group to fast-track your financial goals.

- **Business:** Form strategic alliances, partnerships, or a mastermind that multiplies your reach, insight, and momentum.

The Key: Act Immediately

Don't just identify potential collaborators—reach out now. Send the message. Make the call. Start the conversation today.

Independence can get you started, but synergy is the accelerator—and it only works once you choose to step into it.

Pause here. Look at your list. Every great leap in life or business comes from collaboration—someone who saw further, believed bigger, or walked beside you when it mattered most.

You've built the system. You've expanded your circle. Now it's time to make sure everything you've created stays alive, adaptive, and continually improving.

7. S—Systematically Measure, Reflect, & Adjust

Synergy may accelerate results—but only measurement and reflection can sustain them. Without consistent feedback, even the best systems drift back to old defaults. With it, your success stays alive and keeps compounding.

Think of a long flight: winds nudge the plane off by just one degree, and the autopilot makes tiny corrections so it still lands exactly where intended. Your version of that autopilot—the thing that ensures you reach your results—is a weekly check-in.

Why weekly?

Because fifty-two small course corrections beat twelve monthly reviews—and obliterate a single end-of-year review. Small fixes made early prevent big detours later.

Here's how it works

Schedule 30 minutes at the same day/time each week (Sunday works great) and do the following each time:

1. **Measure what you control.**

   Use a simple scorecard. For each goal, record a 1–10 score (or Yes/No) for the week.

2. **Reflect briefly.**

   On the same scorecard, jot down what worked and what didn't—one line each.

3. **Adjust immediately.**

   Make one small tweak now—update a calendar block, refine a routine, or remove friction.

Rules that keep you focused and on track:

If a score stays low two weeks in a row, don't just push harder. Run the SUCCESS Operating System again from Step 1 and realign.

Within a few weeks of consistent check-ins, clients often report the same shift: control returns—they lead the week instead of chasing it, and progress appears where they've chosen to focus.

Do it now (5 minutes):

1. **Schedule:** Add a 30-minute recurring event at the same day/time each week (Sunday works great). Title it: **Weekly SUCCESS Check-In.**

2. **Create:** Build your one-page scorecard with these fields: **Goal | Score (1–10 or Yes/No) | What worked | What didn't | One adjustment**

Each weekly review sharpens your clarity for the week ahead and strengthens your systems—keeping them aligned with your evolving goals and vision.

Your weekly check-in is the autopilot that keeps you on course. **What you review, you improve.**

Pause here. If you ran the exercises, congratulations—you just installed a complete success cycle. You:

- Took ownership and control of this area

- Unlocked clarity on what truly matters

- Built capacity—inner self-mastery and outer execution

- Chose strategies and goals that actually move the needle

- Installed routines that make the right actions automatic

- Added allies who multiply your momentum

- Set a weekly review that keeps everything on course

If you only read this, don't beat yourself up—but don't kid yourself either. Reading feels *like* progress. Doing *is* progress. Go back, pick one area, and run it now.

Because when you do, you'll notice the shift immediately:

- Momentum replaces pressure.

- Clarity replaces confusion.

- Confidence replaces doubt.

- And results finally start showing up where effort used to disappear.

You've installed it once—but its real power comes when you apply it everywhere.

This 7-step operating system keeps the Entrepreneur $4C^2$ Success Formula fully active—from the foundation to all four core elements.

Apply it next to any area of your life or business:

- **Your business**—scale with clarity and control

- **Your health**—build the energy to perform at your peak

- **Your relationships**—deepen connection and partnership

- **Your friendships**—strengthen a more supportive circle

Each step ties back to the foundation and one or more of the four core elements, keeping all five active, aligned, and working together to drive results.

This is *full integration*, not just inspiration. It doesn't stop at knowing what to do—it ensures you do it, consistently, in the area you've chosen.

How SUCCESS Turns The $4c^2$ Formula Into Results

SUCCESS Step	What it Does	Core $4C^2$ Element(s)	Result You Get
1- Seize Ownership & Control	Shifts you from excuses to full control, putting you in the driver's seat of your results	Foundation	Unshakable Confidence, Inner Certainty & Full Control
2- Unlock Your Inner Compass	Connects your goals to your true values and long-term vision	Create Congruence	Crystal-Clear Vision, Daily Motivation & Laser Focus
3- Cultivate Next-Level Self-Mastery & Execution Skills	Raises your ceiling by building identity, mindset, and emotional skillsets	Cultivate Your Capacity	Unstoppable Growth & Emotional Resilience
4- Create And Implement Effective Strategies & Goals	Transforms your vision into clear strategies and measurable progress	Create Congruence, Cultivate Your Capacity	Tangible Wins, Strategic Clarity & Real Momentum
5- Establish Empowering Systems & Routines	Builds success habits that run automatically—even on your worst days	Commit To Consistency	Sustainable Momentum Without Willpower or Burnout
6- Synergize To Thrive	Multiplies your growth through people, partnerships, and accountability	Champion Collaboration	Exponential Growth Through Strategic Partners
7- Systematically Measure, Reflect, & Adjust	Keeps you focused, aligned, and continuously improving	All 4 Elements	Faster Progress, Sharper Focus & Strategic Adaptability

When even one piece is missing, effort turns into motion without progress—and that's where most entrepreneurs stay stuck. Not from laziness, but from missing links in the system.

Most already excel in one piece of the formula—sometimes two. But the others? They're underdeveloped or ignored. And that gap makes it impossible, no matter how hard you push, to reach the level of success you're truly capable of.

This is why the SUCCESS Operating System exists. It doesn't just amplify your strengths—it ensures *all five* (the foundation plus the four core elements) are active, aligned, and working in harmony every day.

You don't have to fix everything overnight. But you *do* have to stop ignoring what's missing. Because until you do, your results will keep hitting the same ceiling—no matter how much effort you invest.

Let's make it real. After one full run, you'll likely recognize yourself in one of these two patterns:

James: The Connector With No Control

James is charismatic and incredible at building relationships. People love him. He's constantly making deals, forming partnerships, and generating opportunities. On the surface, his business looks like it's thriving—and in many ways, it is.

Behind the scenes? Chaos.

He's missing **Core Element #3: Commit to Consistency.** There are no systems. No reliable processes. Employees churn. Customers complain. James spends most days putting out fires instead of building anything that lasts.

The truth is, James doesn't run a business—he runs a popularity engine trapped inside a pressure cooker.

He's strong in **Core Element #4: Champion Collaboration**, but he's trying to scale chaos. Without consistency anchored to the foundation, collaboration doesn't solve the problem—it only accelerates the mess.

What the SUCCESS Operating System would change:

- **Seize Ownership & Control:** Shift from reacting to directing.

- **Establish Empowering Systems & Routines:** Build repeatable processes that withstand busy seasons and turnover.

- **Systematically Measure, Reflect & Adjust:** Catch breakdowns weekly before they become fires.

Result: Opportunity turns into predictable growth instead of perpetual emergencies.

Me: The Systems Pro Who Couldn't Scale

When I started, I was the opposite of James. My strength was **Core Element #3: Commit to Consistency**. Systems were my superpower. Everything was organized, efficient, and under control. People would walk in and say, *"This runs like a machine."*

The truth? I had success—but the machine wasn't growing.

I was missing **Core Element #4: Champion Collaboration**. I tried to do it all myself. I had structure, but no synergy. No outside fuel. Sales stayed steady. Growth stayed slow.

Then I discovered the **Entrepreneur 4C² Success Formula**—and immediately saw the missing piece. When I began intentionally activating all five pieces (anchored in the foundation of ownership & control), everything changed.

The breakthrough didn't come from working harder—it came from finally working right.

What the SUCCESS Operating System made possible:

- **Synergize to Thrive:** Purposeful partnerships and a stronger circle for fast growth.

- **Systematically Measure, Reflect & Adjust:** Weekly check-ins that compounded momentum.

Result: The business didn't just improve—it took off.

Wherever you recognize a gap, the SUCCESS operating system closes it—because it keeps all five pieces active, aligned, and in motion daily.

So What's the Point?

Most entrepreneurs operate with only part of the formula and try to out-tactic the gap. But sustainable success only happens when all five pieces work together—every day.

That's what the SUCCESS Operating System guarantees. It doesn't add more to your plate; it activates and integrates the foundation and all four core elements so your results stop stalling and start compounding.

You've already learned how each element works—and now you know the system that makes them stick, turning results into something predictable, repeatable, and extraordinary.

Now, keep it in motion.

The Challenge: Keep It Going (Or Do It Now)

You've already run the SUCCESS Operating System once—so don't stop here. Momentum builds through repetition. Each pass makes the system sharper, easier, and faster until it becomes second nature.

If you didn't go through it live earlier, this is your moment. Pick one area of your life or business and run the process from start to finish—right now. Don't overthink it. No skipping. No shortcuts.

If you did complete it live, your next step is simple: keep honoring your Weekly SUCCESS Check-In. Make the tiny weekly changes that remove friction, refine your routines, and sharpen your plan. If a score stays low two weeks in a row, don't push harder—revisit the seven steps, make the adjustment, and return to your weekly loop.

Want next-level results in other areas? After you stabilize wins in your first area, apply the same seven steps to the next—health, relationships, friendships, or anywhere you want to build momentum. Work on one primary area at a time; when it's humming, roll the process forward. The more you use it, the more automatic—and powerful—it gets.

When you do, you'll keep experiencing:

- A vision that pulls you forward

- A plan aligned with who you are

- Routines that make success automatic

- Allies who multiply your momentum

- A weekly "autopilot" that keeps you on course, no matter what life throws your way

You don't need more time; you need a better process. This isn't just a framework; it's your edge: a formula for freedom and a system for growth.

You've built momentum—now it's time to measure it. Because momentum without measurement fades but measured momentum compounds.

Re-baseline in 30 Days

What you measure, you improve. Since you just ran the system, schedule a retake of the Entrepreneur Success Diagnostic 30 days from today. It'll show you exactly how your zones have shifted—what's working, and where to focus next.

Retake it: https://www.MySuccessDiagnostic.com

Or scan this QR code to begin.

Haven't taken it yet? Take it once now—then set your 30-day retake date.

How to use the next 30 days (to raise your Diagnostic scores):

1. **Today:** Run—or rerun—the seven SUCCESS steps start-to-finish on your chosen area.

2. **Each week (for 4 weeks):** Do your weekly review, then quickly re-run the seven steps to realign.

3. **Day 30:** Retake the Diagnostic, compare your scores, and choose your next adjustment.

And remember, your free AI Success Strategist is always there when you need clarity or support. Use it anytime to get unstuck, troubleshoot challenges, or turn adjustments into action.

Run it. Review it. Re-run it. Progress follows what you measure.

This marks the final core chapter of the book. You now have the complete Entrepreneur 4C² Success Formula—and the 7-step SUCCESS Operating System that transforms insight into action, and action into extraordinary results.

What you do with it from here determines everything: the next level of your success, your freedom, and the legacy you'll leave behind.

But before we finish, there's one final decision only you can make:

Will you keep chasing achievements—or finally start building a life of success that's truly yours?

The next chapter won't just wrap up the book—it will invite you to choose your path, once and for all. Achievement might bring results. But **ownership, alignment, capacity, consistency, and collaboration**– that's how you build a life of success.

And one you love living every day.

Let's finish what we started.

CHAPTER 9

Are You Ready for a Life with No Regrets? (Conclusion)

"Your legacy is being written by yourself. Make the right decisions."

— GARY VAYNERCHUK

I was on the floor of my parents' living room, knees pressed into the carpet, my hands driving into my father's chest—counting compressions and silently praying the paramedics would arrive in time. Deep down, I knew he was already gone. But I didn't stop. I kept going—not because I believed I could bring him back, but because I couldn't bear to live with the question, *"What if I had done a little more?"*

As I worked, tears came—not from panic or shock, but from gratitude. Gratitude for the time I hadn't wasted, the healing I had chosen, and the words I hadn't left unsaid. In that moment, I felt something I never expected to feel on a day like that: peace. I had no regrets.

My dad—the man who raised me and helped shape my journey.

Let me back up. My dad's early life was marked by tragedy—his mother was killed when he was young; his father, a sheriff, was accused but never convicted. He grew up in a house of silence and discipline. He carried that forward into the Air Force, and later into our home: high standards, tight control, few words. He provided, but he didn't connect. I left at 18, and for years we kept our distant—occasional, polite contact, nothing more.

After my own rock bottom—bankruptcy, burnout, broken relationships—I decided to rebuild instead of resent. I apologized for my part. I stopped arguing with the dad I wished I'd had and started loving the one I did. I traded holiday updates for simple, consistent touchpoints: Sunday calls, quick texts, short visits. When conversations got hard, I stayed in them; when they got quiet, I stayed present. I asked better questions. I listened longer. And when we needed it, I asked for help.

It wasn't overnight, but we rebuilt. I became the son I wanted to be, and he had space to become the dad I needed. A few years earlier, that day on the carpet would've shattered me with "what ifs." Instead—because we had already done the work—I could grieve without unfinished business.

That peace wasn't an accident. It came from living the very process you've just learned: taking ownership of how I showed up, aligning my actions with the relationship I actually wanted, building the capacity for hard conversations, staying consistent with small, unglamorous touch points, and inviting others into the process when we got stuck. That's the 4C^2 Success Formula in motion—made repeatable by the SUCCESS Operating System. The same work that gave me peace is now in your hands. And now, it's your turn to create that same peace— because you've already installed it once—live—in Chapter 8.

If you've read this far, you're already in rare company. Most people never finish the books they buy. You did—because you're ready to live differently. You've learned the foundation (Take Ownership & Control), the four core elements (Create Congruence, Cultivate Capacity, Commit to Consistency, Champion Collaboration), and the 7-step SUCCESS Operating System that turns ideas into results you can repeat.

But not everyone gets that kind of ending.

A coach friend once told me about a client we'll call Pete—an admired real-estate entrepreneur. On paper, he had it all: deals, reputation, lifestyle. Off paper, he was always "one project away" from being present with his family. He knew something had to change. He even filled out an application to get help—twice. Each time he said, "After this next push." When he finally hired the coach, he died unexpectedly a few days later. No final conversations. No slow mornings with his kids. No chance to build the life he kept postponing.

Pete's story haunts me because it's far more common than we admit. Everyone wants freedom, but most are too busy chasing it to stop and build it. The hardest truth is this: Pete could have kept his business success without the sacrifice—if he'd known a better way and acted on it sooner.

Don't wait for a crisis to make the shift. You already have everything you need: the formula, the system, and this moment.

We started this journey by naming the trap—the Achievement Loop. You've seen why ownership unlocks everything, why "next" never fixes misalignment, why capacity beats time, why routines beat willpower, and why collaboration multiplies everything.

You've come full circle. You now know what a Life of Success truly is—and how to build it. You've learned the foundation of ownership and control, the four core elements that drive extraordinary results, and the system that makes it all real. You've seen how alignment, capacity, consistency, and collaboration work together to create freedom instead of pressure—and, if you followed through in Chapter 8, you've already begun living it.

But here's the truth most will ignore: knowing how isn't enough. You can understand every step, every framework, every strategy—and still drift back into old patterns if you don't decide who you'll be from this moment forward.

The formulas, frameworks, and systems were never the destination—they were the bridge to a new way of leading, living, and loving your life. They gave you tools. What you do next determines whether they become transformation.

Because this isn't just about achieving more. It's about living fully now—*before time, comfort, or circumstance decide for you.* It's about building a life with no regrets—one you're proud to live while you're living it.

And if doubt ever creeps in later, remember that living-room floor. Nothing left unsaid. Nothing left undone. Not perfection—just peace. That's what it means to live a Life of Success.

This is where knowing ends—and deciding begins. So ask yourself the only question that matters—*the one your future self will thank you for answering today:*

Will you keep chasing achievements... or finally start building a Life of Success?

Circle your choice. Date it. Sign it if you have to. Then take your next step—and make this the moment everything changes. Because this is it—the line between intention and transformation.

You've made your choice—or maybe you're staring at the page still deciding. Either way, this is the moment that separates *those who change* from *those who intend to.*

Most people try to do it alone. But the ones who build their Life of Success fastest—the ones who make freedom, fulfillment, and next-level results their reality—don't.

Because clarity without action fades. You don't need another book on your shelf. You need an environment that keeps the system alive, challenges you to grow, and helps you build your Life of Success faster than you ever could alone.

That's exactly why the Next-Level Success Institute exists—the place where entrepreneurs like you *install* what you've just learned, turning alignment into results and momentum into mastery.

If you're ready to turn everything you've learned into massive action and real results, your next move is simple:

Join the Next-Level Success Institute.

This isn't more content—it's an execution environment. Inside, you'll:

- **Get clarity on demand**—guided processes to align every move with your Inner Compass.

- **Make execution inevitable**—simple tools that turn plans into repeatable action.

- **Move faster with support**—timely coaching touchpoints and practical feedback.

- **Level up your circle**—a curated peer group that expands thinking and raises standards.

- **Lock in momentum**—measurement rhythms that keep progress compounding week after week.

- **Continuous upgrades**—resources that evolve as you do. Formats change, the outcomes don't.

Special Reader Advantage: use code **BOOK500** for a $500 credit toward enrollment at the Next-Level Success Institute. Current availability and redemption steps are shown on the enrollment page.

https://www.NextLevelSuccessInstitute.com

Or scan this QR Code:

Prefer a hands-on, high-touch path?

Apply to the Mastery Program (application-only). It combines guided implementation with live one-on-one coaching, small-group work, and targeted feedback—so alignment turns into results, and momentum becomes mastery. This is reserved for those serious about rapid transformation.

Apply at: https://www.NextLevelSuccessInstitute.com/mastery

Or scan this QR code:

Make your choice real. Step in, install it, and build your Life of Success—now.

Don't wait.

Don't let this book just be where it stops. Make it the next step in your evolution.

This isn't the end– It's your beginning.

You have the formula.

You have the system.

You have the power—right now.

This isn't about someday. It's about today.

Now go build your Life of Success—with clarity, with confidence, with courage.

Imagine 6 months from now—waking up each day with peace of mind, purpose in your step, and nothing in your life neglected or on hold.

That's what happens when you live this formula. You won't just grow your business—you'll grow your life.

One you love. One you're proud of.

Success is no longer a mystery.

It's your next move.

Thank you for showing up.

For doing the work.

For choosing a different path.

Writing this book was personal. Living it changed my life. And I truly hope it changes yours.

Here's to your Life of Success—lived fully, led boldly, and without a single regret.

About the Author

Greg is the Founder and Executive Director of the Next-Level Success Institute, a Success Strategist and Mentor to entrepreneurs, a high-energy, passionate speaker, and published author. He helps successful entrepreneurs escape what he calls the 'Achievement Trap'—the cycle of working harder each year while life gets smaller—and build a Life of Success they can look back on with pride and zero regrets.

He's been featured on the cover of *Think Realty* magazine and has appeared in numerous interviews on TV, radio, and podcasts across the country—sharing his insights with audiences looking to grow their business and create a life they love.

With more than 41 years of entrepreneurial experience—including 19 years with McDonald's Corporation, followed by building and scaling multiple successful businesses—Greg brings a powerful blend of corporate discipline and entrepreneurial innovation. He has completed over 1,500 real estate transactions totaling more than \$250 million, making his lessons both practical and proven.

Greg is the creator of the Entrepreneur $4C^2$ Success Formula, a transformative framework distilled from how top-performing entrepreneurs actually operate. He challenges high achievers to think differently, implement smarter systems, and escape the grind-harder mentality that keeps most stuck.

When he's not leading entrepreneurs, you'll find Greg traveling the world with his wife, Kim, or cheering at live sporting events. A firm believer that life is too short not to enjoy it, he brings humor, energy, and passion to everything he does—reminding others to build not just a business, but a life they truly love.

Footnotes:

1. National Sleep Foundation

2. Bank of America Small Business Owner Report

3. Harvard Business Review

4. Michael A. Freeman, UC Berkeley

5. UC Berkeley

6. Kauffman Foundation

7. Guidant Financial

8. National Marriage Project

9. Mohamed El-Erian, Interview with *The Huffington Post*, "Why I Quit My Job as CEO," 2014.

10. Arianna Huffington, *Thrive* (Harmony Books, 2014).

11. Bill Gates, Interview with *The Times*, 2022.

APPENDIX

Start Here: Choose Your Entrepreneur Success Diagnostic

Option A—Online Diagnostic (recommended, 4–7 minutes)

Get instant results and a focused first move to install the SUCCESS Operating System where it will make the biggest difference today.

- Instant zone: Danger, Momentum, or Power

- Personalized first action

- Built-in tracking (retake in 30 days)

- Mobile friendly

Take it now: https://www.MySuccessDiagnostic.com

Option B—In-Book Diagnostic (use if you prefer offline)

If you'd rather stay on paper, begin the full print version below. You'll score each section, identify your zone, and determine your first move without going online.

ENTREPRENEUR SUCCESS DIAGNOSTIC

Before You Begin: Choose One Area to Focus On

To get the most value from this diagnostic, pick one specific area of life or business where you want extraordinary results— but haven't fully achieved them yet.

This could be:

- Your business

- Your health

- A relationship

- Your finances

- Or any area where you feel stuck, frustrated, or unfulfilled

As you answer each question, stay focused on the *one area* you chose.

Your responses will reflect how well you've implemented the Entrepreneur $4C^2$ Success Formula in that part of your life— and where your biggest opportunities for growth are hiding.

This is not a personality diagnostic. It's a clarity tool.

What you're about to take is a diagnostic that reveals how fully you've integrated the five core components that drive next-level success:

1. **Take Ownership & Control**—Taking control of your energy, time, and priorities

2. **Create Congruence**—Aligning vision, business, goals, and daily actions

3. **Cultivate Your Capacity**—Growing into the person your goals require

4. **Commit to Consistency**—Installing systems and routines that run your results

5. **Champion Collaboration**—Fueling growth through aligned partnerships and support

   This diagnostic won't tell you whether your business or marriage is thriving.

   It will tell you whether the operating system you're using is set up to make every individual area of your life thrive or stall.

   Each section has 10 simple but powerful questions. They'll help you uncover where you're strong… and where you're vulnerable to burnout, misalignment, or stalled momentum.

Instructions

- Answer each question honestly based on the one area you've chosen.

- Use this scoring system:

    - Yes = 2 points

    - Sometimes = 1 point

    - No = 0 points

- Total your score for each section.

You can take the diagnostic repeatedly for different areas of your life or business.

Treat it like a mirror—one that doesn't judge, but reflects exactly what to work on next.

Scoring Legend: How to Interpret Your Results

For each section of the Entrepreneur Success Diagnostic, total your score and compare it to the ranges below:

0–10: Danger Zone

You're facing real challenges in this area—but that means it holds your greatest potential for rapid transformation. When you apply the 4C² Success Formula here, progress will often come faster than you think. Start here.

11–16: Momentum Zone

You've made meaningful progress, but gaps, misalignment, or inconsistency are still slowing your results. A few key upgrades could unlock powerful momentum. Fine-tune this area next.

17–20: Power Zone

You've implemented this element of the Formula well. Your habits, strategies, and alignment are strong. Keep refining and use this area as a model for elevating others. Protect and expand it.

Section 1: Taking Ownership & Control

This section reveals whether you're truly leading this area of life—or letting circumstances, emotions, or others take the wheel.

Score each: Yes = 2 | Sometimes = 1 | No = 0

1. Do you take full responsibility for the current results in this area—even if some things feel outside your control?

2. Do you proactively decide what needs to happen each week in this area, rather than reacting to what shows up?

3. Are the goals you're working toward in this area ones you consciously chose—not ones you felt pressured into?

4. Do you consistently make time for this area, even when life gets busy or stressful?

5. When challenges come up here, do you immediately look for solutions—instead of blaming people, systems, or circumstances?

6. Are your daily actions in this area driven by your long-term vision—not just short-term emotions or habits?

7. Do you have clear boundaries that protect this area from distractions, interruptions, or other people's priorities?

8. Are you leading this area with intention—or does it often feel like it's running you?

9. Do you regularly reflect on what's working and what needs to improve in this area—without judgment or avoidance?

10. Have you taken specific steps to eliminate excuses or escape routes that keep you stuck here?

Section 2: Create Congruence

These questions help you assess whether your actions, goals, and structures are aligned with your deeper vision—or pulling you in opposite directions.

Score each: Yes = 2 | Sometimes = 1 | No = 0

1. Is this area of your life moving in the direction you truly want—or drifting by default?

2. Are your goals in this area based on your true vision—or shaped by pressure, ego, or outside influence?

3. Are you emotionally connected to the outcomes you're pursuing in this area?

4. Are your daily actions in this area genuinely aligned with the lifestyle you want long-term?

5. Do you often feel pulled in different directions, like your time and energy don't match what matters most?

6. Do you clearly know what success actually looks like in this part of your life—and are you building toward it?

7. Have you made intentional decisions to align this area of your life with your deeper values and vision?

8. Do you review or reflect regularly to make sure you're on the right path in this area?

9. Are you proud of the progress you're making here—not just externally, but internally too?

10. If nothing changed in this area for the next 12 months, would that feel exciting—or frustrating?

Section 3: Cultivate Your Capacity

This section uncovers how well you're developing the internal mindset, skill sets, and self-mastery needed to grow in this area.

Score each: Yes = 2 | Sometimes = 1 | No = 0

1. Are you actively expanding your skills, mindset, or habits to match your long-term vision in this area?

2. Is this area of your life improving and growing or slowly going in the wrong direction?

3. Are you vigorously developing the specific skills or behaviors needed to create the success you want here?

4. Do you regularly take time to strengthen your ability to stay calm and in control during high-stress moments?

5. Have you hit a ceiling in this area that you can't seem to break through, despite effort or time spent?

6. Do you often feel overwhelmed, underprepared, or like you're just reacting instead of leading?

7. Do you intentionally challenge yourself in ways that stretch your growth here—even when it's uncomfortable?

8. Do your thoughts in this area tend to support your goals—or cause hesitation, doubt, or delay?

9. Is this part of your life improving because of who you're becoming—not just what you're doing?

10. Are you holding yourself accountable for growing into the version of you required to succeed here?

Section 4: Commit to Consistency

These questions examine whether you've built reliable systems and routines—or if you're relying on motivation, willpower, or chaos to get results.

Score each: Yes = 2 | Sometimes = 1 | No = 0

1. Are your results in this area mostly driven by intentional routines—or by reacting to whatever comes up?

2. Do you often start strong but fade quickly when trying to build better habits in this area?

3. Have you installed daily or weekly systems that make success in this area almost automatic?

4. Do your current habits in this area consistently support your long-term goals?

5. Have you ever hit a wall here—not because of lack of effort, but because your systems couldn't keep up?

6. Do you rely more on motivation or willpower than proven routines and structure?

7. Have you recently made small, strategic upgrades to improve the way you operate here?

8. Do your mornings or evenings consistently include habits that reinforce this part of your life?

9. Do you regularly track, review, or reflect on what's working and what's not in this area?

10. When life gets busy or stressful, do your systems still carry you forward in this area—or do things fall apart?

Section 5: Champion Collaboration

This section evaluates whether you're working with others to accelerate progress—or trying to do it all alone, leading to slow or stalled results.

Score each: Yes = 2 | Sometimes = 1 | No = 0

1. Do you intentionally build relationships in this area that align with your goals and values?

2. Are you currently trying to do too much alone—even though support could accelerate your progress?

3. Have you clearly communicated your vision in this area to people who could help you?

4. Do you regularly seek out people who challenge, inspire, or expand your thinking in this area?

5. Have you ever plateaued or burned out in this area because you lacked the right people around you?

6. Do you proactively create win-win collaborations or partnerships—not just wait for them to appear?

7. Are you surrounded by people in this area who push you to grow, lead, or live at a higher level?

8. When facing a challenge here, do you reach out for help—or default to handling it all yourself?

9. Have you recently invested time, energy, or resources into strengthening your support system here?

10. Are you building this part of your life with aligned people—or mostly trying to figure it out solo?

Optional: Overall Score Snapshot

Want a big-picture overview of how well you've implemented the Formula?

Add together the total scores from all five sections to get a single score out of 100.

This gives you a snapshot of your overall alignment and readiness for next-level success in the area you diagnosed.

These zones mirror the same categories used in each section—so your full score reflects your total integration of the Formula.

0–50: Danger Zone

You're working hard, but without the right foundation. Huge growth potential—but big changes are needed.

51–80: Momentum Zone

You're doing a lot right, but still missing key elements that are holding you back. Focused upgrades can unlock serious momentum.

81–100: Power Zone

You've implemented most of the Formula. Keep refining, reinforcing, and using this area as a model for others.

Once you've finished the diagnostic for your chosen area, you can use it again anytime you want to grow another part of your life or business.

The Formula doesn't change but where you apply it will.

So whether it's your health, finances, relationships, or leadership… just come back, pick a new focus, and run the diagnostic again.

You can revisit this diagnostic again and again as you grow.

Use it to track your progress, re-evaluate different areas, and keep yourself aligned.

Treat it like a mirror—one that doesn't judge, but reflects exactly what to focus on next.

You don't need to fix everything at once.

Just identify your gaps… and put the Formula to work. That's how next-level success begins—right now, in the area that needs it most.

Bonus Resources

As a thank-you for reading, here are **two powerful tools** to help you implement what you've learned and create extraordinary results faster:

1. Free Next-Level Success Diagnostic (4–7 minutes)

Get an instant, personalized snapshot across Ownership & Control, Create Congruence, Cultivate Capacity, Commit to Consistency, and Champion Collaboration—plus your current zone (Danger, Momentum, or Power) with a tailored action prompt. The online version is continuously updated and goes deeper than the appendix version.

▶ Start now: https://www.MySuccessDiagnostic.com

Or Scan the QR code below:

2. GregSlaughterAI—Your 24/7 Success Strategist

Stuck? Curious? Need quick insight on applying the 4C² Success Formula or the SUCCESS Operating System to your life or business? Ask GregSlaughterAI anytime for on-demand guidance and next steps.

▶ Visit: https://www.NextLevelSuccessInstitute.com/ai

Or Scan the QR code below:

www.ingramcontent.com/pod-product-compliance
Lightning Source LLC
Chambersburg PA
CBHW041316120726
48005CB00014B/2016